Butterflies Are Free...What About Me:

One Woman's Battle With Anorexia Nervosa

By Wendy R. Levine

DEDICATION

Dedicated with love to my wonderful parents, Beverly Levine and the late George Levine (my hero). They stood by me in the darkest hours of my struggle.

Table of Contents

Foreword

Working in the field of eating disorders (EDs) is both rewarding and draining. To see those you care about go through such a devastating illness is heartbreaking. To have your whole world controlled by food is exhausting. From the moment you wake up to the moment you go to sleep, it's what's on your mind: "What should I eat, what am I supposed to stay away from, how much do I need to exercise to get rid of what I ate, and what happens when I don't stick to the plan?" Can you imagine how much time is spent thinking about these things and the anxiety, guilt, and anger that comes with not giving in to that voice, and even the anxiety that comes with not doing exactly what your support system tells you to do? There are feelings of guilt for disappointing yourself or others who are just trying to help you. It's almost easier to just give in, which is why this illness hijacks so many and has the highest mortality rate of any other mental illness. And no one is immune. Eating disorders do not discriminate. They affect the young, the old, the privileged, the less fortunate, and even those without underlying issues. Those who it impacts may come in many different shapes and sizes, but I'm sure anyone who has struggled and/or has watched someone struggle can agree that the eating disorder itself is one size fits all: miserable. Or, as Wendy puts it, it's like being stuck in a metaphorical prison with the key, but unable to use it. That's how manipulative and debilitating the disease can be.

On the other side of it, you get to work with people like Wendy—an individual who has battled this monster for 47-plus years, who has now made it her life's work to give back, educate, and put her story on display. ED would not be too happy about this. Rather than giving in and shutting down, Wendy lets go and speaks out. She is still on her road to recovery, but has a message that is sure to help herself and others fully recover. No matter how old or how young, recovery is possible. The road you take will likely be unique and it won't always be easy, but it is possible. Wendy now uses her voice to help others, rather than allowing the ED voice that manipulates, isolates, and discriminates to be her voice. It is definitely a daily battle, but one she has the strength and courage to fight and the willingness to eventually conquer.

For those who struggle, Wendy's story is both real and relatable. It's interesting to hear the echo of her experience, which started so many years ago, in the young men and women I work with today. It's also sad because although there are many more recovery options and resources, the voice of comparison and self-judgment still have so much power. Idealistic images still reign and in some ways are even more present and definitely more available. This is why Wendy's story is so important and so pertinent. It shows the history of eating disorders as it relates to present day and the oh-so-common similarities. It also shows tremendous vulnerability in a world that can be so judgmental. I thank Wendy for giving me the opportunity to be a part of her story and look forward to her continued growth and recovery as she beats the odds.

Mari W. Broome, LCSW, RYT-200, RCY

Licensed Clinical Social Worker

Why I Wrote This Book

Very often when one has a passion in life they pursue it with as much vigor as humanly possible. For me that passion is anorexia nervosa, an insidious eating disorder which has plagued me for over 47 years. As I reflect upon what I have done with my life, I feel a sense of disappointment. I know that if anorexia nervosa wasn't the forefront of my life for so long, I could have enjoyed and accomplished much more than I have. Although there is no turning back for me, I am hopeful that by sharing my experiences with others, perhaps I can help prevent someone else from experiencing the pain I have known. As I embarked on the venture of writing this book, I knew that it wouldn't be easy as I'd be reliving some of the pain and agony. However, if I can prevent even one person from the suffering that is inherent in anorexia nervosa and related eating disorders, the difficulty will have been well worth it.

The key to attacking eating disorders is to hone in on the triggers and make certain that we do not in any way perpetuate them. For example, I would never tell a young child that they are *"too heavy"* for me to pickup and carry. Rather, I might say something like, "you are becoming too grown up for me to carry around." What you say can hurt and leave scars that will last a lifetime. I know this first hand.

I truly believe that if people are informed and are willing to make changes in what we value as "beauty," then there is a chance anorexia nervosa and related eating disorders can be prevented.

I want to make it clear from the outset that my anorexia nervosa was not the direct result of any one incident or person. As I view it, the seeds of the illness were sown early in my life in a variety of situations. The illness took root, and because of the values in our society, it was able to grow out of control. In this book, I have attempted to candidly share some of those experiences with you.

Watch What You Say: Regardless of circumstances *never, ever tell* **an Anorexic that they look good**. As innocent and well-intentioned as this statement may be, they will hear it as they are looking FAT!!! Rather than focus on general appearance, tell them that you like the shirt they are wearing or the way they have done their hair.

Anorexia Nervosa: Overview from the National Eating Disorders Association

Anorexia nervosa is an eating disorder characterized by weight loss (or lack of appropriate weight gain in growing children); difficulties maintaining an appropriate body weight for height, age, and stature; and, in many individuals, distorted body image. People with anorexia generally restrict the number of calories and the types of food they eat. Some people with the disorder also exercise compulsively, purge via vomiting and laxatives, and/or binge eat.

Anorexia can affect people of all ages, genders, sexual orientations, races, and ethnicities. Historians and psychologists have found evidence of people displaying symptoms of anorexia for hundreds or thousands of years. People in non-Westernized areas, such as rural China and Africa, have also been diagnosed with anorexia nervosa.

Although the disorder most frequently begins during adolescence, an increasing number of children and older adults are also being diagnosed with anorexia. Nor does a person need to be emaciated or underweight to have anorexia. Studies have found that larger-bodied individuals can also have anorexia, although they may be less likely to be diagnosed due to cultural prejudice against fat and obesity.

To be diagnosed with anorexia nervosa according to the DSM-5, the following criteria must be met:

1. Restriction of energy intake relative to requirements leading to a significantly low body weight in the context of age, sex, developmental trajectory, and physical health.

2. Intense fear of gaining weight or becoming fat, even though underweight.

3. Disturbance in the way in which one's body weight or shape is experienced, undue influence of body weight or shape on self-

evaluation, or denial of the seriousness of the current low body weight.

Even if all the DSM-5 criteria for anorexia are not met, a serious eating disorder can still be present. Atypical anorexia includes those individuals who meet the criteria for anorexia but who are not underweight despite significant weight loss. Research studies have not found a difference in the medical and psychological impacts of anorexia and atypical anorexia.

Brief History of Anorexia Nervosa

Though most people consider anorexia nervosa a relatively new disease, a look at history and literature confirm that indeed, the disorder was apparent as far back as the Victorian era.

The term anorexia nervosa was coined by William Gull, an English physician, in 1868. In 1873, French psychiatrist Charles Lasegue documented the disease in his book, *L'Anorexie Hysterique*.

Lasegue identified three stages of anorexia:

- Stage One: Feeling a generalized "uneasiness"—after eating, a young woman would begin to reduce her intake of food.

- Stage Two: The afflicted individual would become obsessed and focus totally on food and how little she could eat.

- Stage Three: Medical help sought only when the patient's physical deterioration became evident to family and friends.

Much like today's society in which it is often thought a woman can never be "too rich or too thin," women in the Victorian era lived with the idea that a healthy appetite or desire for food might be equated with a desire for sex.

As we tackle the problem of anorexia nervosa in the 21st Century, we see that today "there is nothing new under the sun."

In chapter two of her book, *Fasting Girls*, Joan Jacobs Brumberg reveals that in medieval Europe, particularly between 1200 and 1500, prolonged fasting by women was considered a "female miracle." Brumberg also tells the stories of many women saints who "ate almost nothing or claimed to be incapable of eating normal earthly fare." Brumberg describes:

"In the medieval period fasting was fundamental to the model of female holiness. The medieval woman's capacity for survival

without eating meant that she found other forms of food: prayer provided sustenance, as did the Christian eucharist."

According to Brumberg, starving women during the High Middle Ages were said to be suffering from "inedia prodigiosa (a great starvation) or anorexia miriabilis (miraculously inspired loss of appetite)."

Though we have much documentation that what today is referred to as anorexia nervosa has been around for quite some time, it is rather shocking to learn that in the United States, the first published photo of a girl suffering from anorexia nervosa was on October 5, 1932 in an issue of the *New England Journal of Medicine*.

Looking back upon my personal history with anorexia, I cannot help but wonder what my life would be like had the medical community in the 1970s been schooled in this disorder which is by no means a new disease.

Annual Physical aka Introduction into World of Dieting

Under the best of circumstances, the transition from childhood to adolescence can be difficult. For me, the one incident that stands out during this "passage of life" was my annual physical exam the summer preceding eighth grade. Not only do I vividly remember the defining incident, but I can tell you exactly what I was wearing as well: a yellow* floral print sleeveless dress that I made during the sewing segment of seventh grade home economics class.

After examining me, the doctor said that when I got dressed he would like to talk to me and my mother in the waiting room. Lucky me, I was the last appointment of the day and except for the doctor, my mom, and myself, the four walls were the only ears privy to the conversation. Stating that I was somewhat overweight for my age, he handed us a copy of a paperback booklet entitled "A Girl and Her Figure." Although I don't remember exactly what the yellow* colored booklet said, I do know that this was my introduction to the world of "dieting."

Yes, my mother tried to "curb my appetite," but I truly wasn't interested in dieting at this point in my life. Although I was never "obese" and did dabble in dieting from time to time, I continued to wear my extra pounds until my junior year of high school.

*To this day, I dislike the color yellow and go out of my way to avoid purchasing anything yellow, whether it be for me or a gift for someone else!

Jerry K.'s Remark

What's your favorite part of a cookout? As a child, mine was toasting marshmallows with my brothers, until one day when I suddenly lost my taste for the crisp gooey morsel. No, my marshmallow didn't get charred by the hot coals, but the hurt I experienced that day was as painful as if I had burned my hand while toasting the delicious treat.

Again, for whatever it's worth, I can tell you exactly what I was wearing when the pain hit: navy blue cotton pants with a faint white pinstripe, a red belt, and a white short sleeved shirt. The weather provided a picture-perfect New England day—a blue sky and bright sunshine coupled with the distinct smell of a barbecue.

Everything was going along fine until one of my parents' guests made a comment that hit me like a bolt of lightning. Jerry, who was standing with my parents and some other adults, had the chutzpah to ask my parents, "how is it that you have two sons who are thin and a daughter who is fat?" Upon hearing the query put forth by this ill-mannered man, I dropped my toasting stick (marshmallow and all) into the grill and ran into the house. Once inside, I headed for the living room couch where I buried my face into the cushion and cried my heart out. How could such a wonderful day have been ruined in a split second? In an attempt to coax me back outside, my brother Barry (always my loyal champion) came in and said, "He's just a stupid old man, forget it." Forget it, I could not. Today, some 45 years later, the pain and humiliation are still present.

Feeling badly about the situation, Jerry himself came into the living room to extend an apology. In fact, each time Jerry and his wife Marion saw me after this debacle, they almost always made it a point to comment that I looked like I "had lost some weight." Alas, these two people are dead, yet to this day I can't look at a marshmallow without thinking about *that day*.

Metrecal for Lunch Bunch

Coming of age in the 60s was very different than it is today. In addition to TV sets without remote controls and 33 LP albums, we had the "Metrecal for Lunch" bunch. Though I personally wasn't a member of this group, I was witness to my mother's participation. Truthfully, as a child I don't recall my mom being "fat." But she must have been (!?!) for she and some of her friends watched exercise with Jack LaLanne and then drank their Metrecal for lunch. Was Metrecal the Slimfast of the 60s? I don't know how the two weight control drinks compare but I do remember my mom and her friends comparing one flavor to another.

Although I never partook of Metrecal, my mom and I attempted "dieting" together during my early teen years. Today, for some reason, the one single incident about this attempt at dieting that I remember is the time we "cheated" together. Hungry and feeling deprived (I suppose), we went through the kitchen cabinet until we found something appealing: a wafer-type cookie coated in chocolate. My mom assured me that we deserved this treat and would feel much better after we got something good to eat. How did I feel? I really don't know. But once again, the incident sticks out as one of the moments of bonding with mom. Feh!!

Jewish Grandmothers and Food

Stereotypically, Jewish mothers and grandmothers, among other things, are depicted as stuffing their offspring with food. For anyone raised in the "tradition," the phrase "ess mein kin" (eat, my child) is no doubt a familiar refrain.

Unfortunately, my paternal grandmother, Sarah, died while I was an infant and I have absolutely no first-hand recollections of her. From stories that have been passed on through others who knew her, I envision a strong woman who sacrificed for her family during rough times.

I do have many fond memories of my maternal grandmother, Anna. She was a petite woman with the patience of Job. As I recall, she acted as model for my brother when he was learning the major bones of the body in his physiology class. Patiently, she stood or sat as he displayed his breadth of knowledge using her as a model. On a personal level, I fondly remember grandma as being the only person who would rub my back for as long as I wanted. Because she and my grandfather lived in the Bronx, New York, and we lived in Worcester, Massachusetts, there was often considerable time between visits. But, no matter, grandma was my personal back rubber! Ah, what a wonderful feeling. Grandma and grandpa also spoiled us whenever possible. On several occasions I remember grandma saying in Yiddish, "let her have a shtikel (small bit)" of whatever. However, one day, even grandma became the "enemy" when I was eating fresh bakery rye bread as a snack. She bluntly reminded me that I was supposed to be "curbing my appetite." Ouch—a big hurt coming from someone whom I loved dearly.

Brotherly Love

As the only girl and youngest child in a family of three children, I felt cheated. While my brothers seemed to always have one another, I felt left out. Wish as I might, a sister was not in the offing for me. Today, as I think about the days when I would have traded one of my brothers for a sister, I can honestly say that I would no more trade one of them than I would the beautiful hazel green eyes I have been blessed with. As we mature, our values change, and I am truly grateful for having been blessed with my older brother Barry.

Of course, this is not to say that there are moments I wouldn't want to erase. Historically, older brothers take special delight in tormenting their little sisters—I have learned this after much discussion with other "little sisters," including my sister-in-law Pam. I have countless stories of "torment" perpetrated by my brothers in their endeavor to express their love. Perhaps the most painful of my reminiscences is a little ditty they sang to me: "Tubby tubby two by four, couldn't fit through the bathroom door, so she made it on the floor." Hurtful, yes. But did my brothers really mean to cause me such pain? No! I only cite this instance as yet another example of how words can and do hurt others despite intentions. Though I knew and still know they love me, a picture is worth a thousand words and unfortunately, I still have this picture etched in my memory.

So Close, Yet, So Far

Clinical experience and research have shown that the sooner anorexia nervosa and related eating diseases are diagnosed and addressed, the greater the chances for recovery.

When I first began my battle with anorexia nervosa at the age of 16 ½ (1971), little, if anything, was publicly available about the eating disorder. I believe that many factors (including genetics) contributed to my affliction with the disease. I would like to again stress that it wasn't any single factor or incident which caused my anorexia. As far as I'm concerned there are no guilty parties in my longtime battle with anorexia, except perhaps for a therapist in Upstate New York who had an inkling of what was going on and used this knowledge to his own advantage.

When I was a junior in high school my family moved from Worcester, Massachusetts, a fairly large city, to Tillson, New York, a rural community nestled among scenic views in the mid-Hudson Valley. The move was necessitated by the fact that the City of Worcester, in its urban renewal efforts, took the property on which my dad's store was located. Having two children in college and another not far behind, my parents were forced to make a move none of us were happy about. Each member of my family suffered as a result of this move.

As a teenager, my life in Worcester was not idyllic, but it was familiar. In addition to my involvement with the synagogue and its youth group, I had a small circle of friends. When we moved, I lost these familiar comforts. Quiet and on the shy side by nature, I wasn't looking forward to carving out a new life for myself at the tender age of 16 ½. At home I rebelled at every moment I could and reminded my parents how miserable I was. Absorbed in myself, I failed to see how miserable they were too.

The first day of my junior year as a student at Kingston High School was almost my last. With great difficulty, during homeroom period, I introduced myself to the girl sitting next to me and explained that I was a new student. Her response of "so what" was shocking. The rest of that day was pretty uneventful except for my business law teacher who lashed into me for being late to class. Kingston High School was a large urban school with a main building and several annexes. This teacher had no sympathy for any student, new or old, who dared show up late for her class.

On the second day of school when I was once again late for my business law class, this teacher threatened me—and that's when I reached the breaking point. I returned home from school and told my parents that if I were to complete my high school education, it would have to be through a correspondence course. Poor mom and dad, not only did they have their own misery to deal with but also mine. My mom related my tale of woe to Mrs. F., a neighbor across the street, who assured her that everything would be ok. At that time the family had five daughters, four of school age, all of whom attended Catholic schools. Mr. and Mrs. F. told my parents that they knew that I was going to have difficulty making the transition from my school in Massachusetts to Kingston, HS. Unbeknownst to us, prior to school starting, they consulted with their priest and wheels were set in motion. My parents and I were invited to come and interview with Sr. Mary Rose, principal at John A. Coleman Catholic High School (JAC). Reluctantly, mom and I went to see what JAC was all about. Unlike the public school, this private Catholic School was housed in a fairly new and modern facility.

Although I'm not 100% sure how I got from the interview to matriculating as the first Jewish student to walk the halls of JAC, the next two years of my life were spent trying to uphold the notion that "Jewish people are bright academic achievers." During the course of my two-year stint at JAC, I experienced anti-Semitism on many levels from students and several faculty members. The horror of dealing with those two years could be its own book, but for now suffice it to say the experience was a rude awakening. Of course, not all of the people I encountered at JAC were "mean spirited" regarding Jews, but I certainly had my fair share of hurdles to overcome.

During this time, I decided that I was going to remake myself: lose weight and let my stick straight short hair grow long. I proceeded on a very spare diet and by the end of senior year was being called "twiggy." Though I did not feel that I looked "OK," I did receive much praise for paring my body down. Again hurtful, but true, is a comment my friend Susan from Worcester made regarding my weight loss. She told me that she was proud of my accomplishment but that I still looked matronly because of my large bust. To this day I believe she was in no way trying to hurt me. But words stick, and although they cannot break our bones, they can break our spirit. I vowed to lose more weight. Throughout my academic career at the State University of New York at New Paltz, I maintained my weight loss and in addition to my studies focused exclusively on food, calories, the scale and body image.

After graduating from college, I began seeing a psychologist who was recommended by our family physician. The diagnosis was depression. While in the course of therapy, I worked as a feature writer for the *Huguenot Herald*, a weekly newspaper in New Paltz, New York.

When Stephen R., a practical jokester and editor of the *Huguenot Herald*, told me that I was to interview Isaac Asimov the next day, I blew the assignment off as one of his jokes. However, when he insisted that I get a front-page story, I called Mohonk Mountain House at Lake Mohonk in New Paltz and was told that "Mr. Asimov was not setting up advance meetings with the press, I'd have to try to catch him between lectures." Although I was familiar with the name, Isaac Asimov, I had no clue as to what he was all about. I made a trip to the library and checked out several books about, and by, Asimov. After spending a good portion of the evening and early morning hours reading about Asimov, I felt as ready as one could to interview such a man.

I arrived at Lake Mohonk early enough to get a good seat for Asimov's lecture. After the author's talk, I shyly made my way over to him and introduced myself as Wendy Levine, a reporter from the local newspaper, the *Huguenot Herald*. At age 21, I was in a room full of Asimov fans and reporters from newspapers including the *New York Times* and *Post*. I don't know if it was beginner's luck or just that Asimov was intrigued by the "kid reporter" from the local press but he promised me an exclusive interview after lunch. I was excited and nervous. But what should have been a thrilling occasion became more like a nightmare. For whatever reason, I was invited to sit at Asimov's table and declined because I was terrified of having to eat in front of him. Imagine, I actually said no to "breaking bread" with a famous author! Rather, I sat at the Press table trying to act confident among seasoned reporters, while trying to avoid the meal being served. Although I don't recall what was being served, I do know that at that point in my illness I was not able to eat in front of other people and relied on various "excuses" for not partaking of food being served. After lunch I did get my personal interview with Asimov—a front page story (my first!).

At this time in my life, socializing was minimal due to my as-yet-undiagnosed eating disorder. When I was invited to an event where food was part of the offing, I invariably used one of my standby excuses—stomachache, toothache, etc.—to avoid the whole event or at least the food. This is why I, a loving person who values friends as one of life's most precious gifts, have absolutely no friends from college days. My only "friends" during this period of my life were the scale, calorie charts, exercise bike and other accoutrements related to weight loss.

Perhaps the saddest incident I remember regarding the early days of my eating disorder is a visit to our family doctor's office. As is customary in many medical practices, the nurse or medical assistant recorded my vital signs and weight prior to the doctor seeing me. On this particular visit, the medical assistant asked me to step on the scale. When I said I'd rather not, she somehow cajoled me into obedience and announced that my weight was 112. At this news, I remember crying, "*it should be lower with all the laxatives I took!!*" Today, if someone were to utter those words under similar circumstances, I am certain they would be heard. However, in my case, we were talking about the mid-1970s before eating disorders were a public item. How unfortunate for me, as I truly believe that if my anorexia nervosa had been diagnosed at an earlier stage, I would now be enjoying life without vestiges of the disease.

Stumbling Block

When an individual has low self-esteem they often look for ways to "prove" to themselves why they are not up to par. For me, this was a recurring pattern. However, on one occasion it backfired and I used anorexia nervosa as my ticket out.

While working after college at the *Huguenot Herald*, I learned that Rotary International was awarding 35 scholarships worldwide to individuals interested in pursuing graduate work in journalism in a foreign country. For me, this was an ideal situation to reinforce my sense of "worthlessness."

Inasmuch as I am not fluent in any language other than English, I decided that I would apply for a scholarship to study at a university in Great Britain. I contacted the local Rotary Club in New Paltz, New York, and they agreed to sponsor me. After completing an in-depth application, including autobiography, I waited several months before learning that my application had been selected and I was invited to participate in the second round. This next stage included an interview with other candidates and Rotarians, and a luncheon in Newburgh, New York.

Aside from being nervous about the interview itself, I carried the extra baggage of my eating disorder to the table. While the other candidates and Rotarians enjoyed lunch, I sat there saying that I was "suffering from a stomach bug" and couldn't possibly get down more than a cup of tea. I figured this excuse was as good as any since I'd probably never see these people again. After the luncheon and interview, there was a hiatus of several months before I heard anything from Rotary International.

Much to my shock, I received a thick envelope in the mail congratulating me on receiving one of the coveted scholarships. The letter stated that due to funding, they were able to award a total of 70 journalism scholarships worldwide. Did this mean my scholarship was only half as good? I remember being elated yet feeling I had dug a hole for myself. I could not possibly have been more confused at that point. How could I, a mere nebbish, have won such a prestigious scholarship? Could I even accept the award? To outright deny it would have lead people to believe I was insane. So, after sharing the news with my family, friends, and journalism professor Leland E. Heinze, I headed for the library to see what type of culinary delights the people of Great Britain enjoyed.

A few weeks later, as an invited guest at the New Paltz Rotary weekly luncheon at Dominick's Restaurant in New Paltz, New York, I stood before a roomful of Rotarians and thanked them for granting me this chance of a lifetime. The president of the local group presented me with several flags, which I was expected to deliver to Rotary groups abroad as I carried out my functions as "Ambassador of Good Will."

I applied for and received my passport, corresponded with my host family, and purchased a good camera and luggage. However, when push came to shove, I reluctantly informed my sponsoring Rotary group that "due to illness in my family," I would be unable to accept the scholarship.

At this point, keep in mind, my eating disorder had not been identified and I was not in treatment. Although I knew that something was terribly wrong, I did not know I was caught up in the throes of a life-threatening disease.

Embarrassed and feeling ever much a loser, I decided to move to Boston, Massachusetts where I could forget about the scholarship debacle. Though I was back in my beloved Massachusetts, I did not leave behind my sense of worthlessness or my eating disorder. It would be several more years before my eating disorder was given a name and I would begin treatment.

Therapy in New Paltz

During my junior or senior year of college, our family doctor in Upstate New York suggested that I consult with a colleague of his, a psychologist who was also a professor at a university in New York State. Realizing that I was depressed, I reluctantly made an appointment.

During my sessions, discussion pretty much focused on how fat I felt. Through our discussions and my behavior, this therapist was able to ascertain that I had low self-esteem, was sexually inexperienced, and pretty much afraid of my own shadow. To help me with all this he suggested desensitization exercises. Although my anorexia had not been diagnosed at this point in time, I truly believe that this psychologist suspected I had an eating disorder and used this to "take advantage of me and engage in unorthodox therapy." Part of the eating disorder is a fear of fat; for me this manifested itself to the extreme that I didn't want to be hugged by family lest they feel the fat. The therapist began "touch therapy" by standing behind me and placing his hand on my shoulder. I tensed, and he just kept his hand there. Without graphically spelling it out, suffice it to say his hands eventually touched my most private parts. He explained this was necessary if I were ever to be an adult and not a "babe in the woods." What he did was wrong, but for a long time, I felt that I too was wrong for letting him try to help me like this. It was not until many years later when I was in treatment for anorexia nervosa that I shared what happened with anyone. Although the therapist I shared this with wrote a letter to the Board of Psychologists in New York State, there was nothing that could be done so many years after the fact.

Why do I think this practitioner knew I was suffering from anorexia nervosa? He loaned me a book to read, *The Golden Cage*, written by

Hilde Bruch, the world's foremost authority on eating disorders during that time. I remember identifying with Alma, the book's main character, and discussing this with him. I can't change what happened, but I do believe that a great injustice occurred during the course of my treatment in New York State.

Finally, a Referral...

Although I had left New York State, my anorexia nervosa and the memories of therapy traveled to Massachusetts with me. Again, not knowing what was wrong with me (i.e. anorexia) I sought therapy to try to deal with my issues. For approximately one year I worked with a female psychologist in Brookline, Massachusetts. Although I never spoke about the therapy I had in New York, I was constantly talking about fat, food, calories, etc. At some point, she informed me that she was concerned that I was suffering from anorexia nervosa, a disorder she had no experience treating. However, she had made some phone calls and was referring me to David Herzog, a psychiatrist at Massachusetts General Hospital, who was knowledgeable about eating disorders. (Today, Dr. Herzog is known internationally for his work with eating disorders.) My kind therapist in Brookline was careful not to make me feel as if she were rejecting me—she truly was concerned that she could not give me the help I needed.

My consultation with Dr. Herzog ended in a referral to Christopher Gordon, M.D., another Mass General doctor who dealt with eating disorders. During the many years that I was in therapy with Dr. Gordon, he became someone I hated, respected, feared, loved, tolerated and was grateful for having in my life. He yelled at me, laughed with me, cried with me, visited me when I was hospitalized, threatened to stop therapy, referred me to Dr. Charles Welch for my major depression, met with my family, recommended family therapy and finally...he and his wife Julie danced at my wedding on August 12, 2000.

Again, I cannot stress the importance of early diagnosis and intervention for the successful treatment of anorexia nervosa and other eating disorders. By the time I began treatment with Dr. Gordon, my anorexia nervosa had taken firm root and would not simply "go away." There were several times that I believed I might die from the anorexia but at the same time didn't know a way out of the illness. I expected Dr. Gordon would show me the way out. Well, therapy is a lot of work and it doesn't always end in a cure. Though I had come light years from when I first met Dr. Gordon, when I decided to end therapy, I was not fully recovered. However, Dr. Gordon's persistence and "unconditional love" are part of the reason I am here today. I truly believe he did as much for me as was humanly possible. Though there were many times I got angry with him (and he with me), he was *there* for me. I am thankful to Dr. Gordon for believing in me even when I didn't believe in myself.

My first visit to a nutritionist was during the course of my therapy with Dr. Gordon when he referred me to the Nutrition Service at Mass General. Miriam ("Mim") Seidel, an energetic young woman, was the nutritionist assigned to me. Being close in age we bonded fairly well, and I enjoyed seeing her except for getting weighed. Mim was tough but she was also sensitive to the struggle I was experiencing. Although she refused to share my recipe for hot chocolate with her other patients, (add cocoa and sweet n' low or other non-sugar sweetener to hot water), I felt she respected me as a person. On days when I was to be weighed by her I wore the same clothing. Because my appointments were generally in the early evening after work, I did not eat or drink during the day prior to my appointment. Mim stressed the importance of not engaging in these behaviors, but I was not able to take her advice. Getting weighed was necessary because if my weight dropped below a certain number, hospitalization would be immediate. When the seasons changed and colder weather settled in, Mim bent the rules and let me leave my thin cotton dress in her office so I could continue wearing it when I was weighed. Before stepping on the scale, I would change into the dress which helped lessen my anxiety. Although Mim knew much about me, I knew little about her other than her boyfriend's name was Dave and she lived in Somerville, a city outside of Boston.

Mim and I weren't yet friends in the traditional sense, but I trusted her and would have liked to have worked with her longer. However, one day when I came in for my appointment she told me that she and Dave were moving out of state and my case was going to be transferred to a woman by the name of Carole. Because it was not advisable for "care givers" to remain in touch with patients, Mim and I said a tearful goodbye. Shortly before Mim's marriage to Dave, I gave a card to Carole to forward to her. Much to my surprise and delight, Mim acknowledged the card and included her address. We have been communicating ever since and I attended the Bat Mitzvah of her daughter Naomi, and Mim and Dave were at my wedding.

Hospitalizations in The 1980s

Anorexia Nervosa

My battle with anorexia nervosa was by no means easy. Along with the anorexia came an unrelenting major depression. On several occasions I was hospitalized in an eating disorders unit to fight the battle. However, when the depression became so debilitating that I could not handle it, I was hospitalized for both major depression and the anorexia.

Being an anorexic patient in a unit comprised of other anorexics and bulimics makes for some interesting interactions. Although we were categorized as either "A menu" patients or "B menu" patients, during therapy it soon became apparent that whether one was suffering from the horrors of anorexia or bulimia, our respective roots were similar. The biggest difference I recall was that the anorexics were constantly looking for ways to minimize the portions they were served, while the bulimic patients wished for larger portions. Through various therapies (individual, group, art, creative, cooking, journaling and relaxation) we attempted to confront our illness at every level. Depending upon one's situation, one either ate three meals and three snacks daily or had the added bonus of an Ensure nightcap. Though the rules and regulations that we had to abide by seemed strict and demeaning at times, they were necessary to keep each patient on track. Avoiding any possible discrepancies, we had weigh-in before breakfast, clad in a hospital gown. This was done to ensure that there would be no water weighting or hiding items in lingerie. Meals were generally eaten in the group room with several monitors watching our every move. In the event that one did not finish their meal in full, the penalty was having to drink a serving of Carnation Instant Breakfast. After the torture of eating, we had "porch time" where we wrote in our journals (some of my writings are included in this book).

Major Depression

As if fighting anorexia nervosa was not enough, I also had to surmount a battle with several episodes of major depression. Although it is not uncommon for those suffering with eating disorders to have a dual diagnosis of depression, the depth of my depression was so deep that at some intervals, medications were ineffective at lifting the cloud of despair. It was on these occasions that the "big guns" were brought out and electric convulsive therapy (ECT) was employed to bring me back to the world of the "living." Before you make a judgment call and say "boy, she must have been crazy," let me assure you that ECT is not used on "crazy" people. For me and many other individuals in the depths of a deep and dark depression, ECT can be a true life-saver administered on an inpatient or outpatient basis. My first course of ECT was performed while I was an inpatient at Massachusetts General Hospital by Dr. Charles Welch, a truly wonderful man who never gave up hope that the beast could be beaten.

Writings, Etc. During Hospitalizations

April 17, 2017

For some reason when writing this book, I nearly forgot about the journal I kept while in treatment three times at Fairwinds Treatment Center in Clearwater, Florida.

On Saturday, April 15, 2017 when thinking about my life and the book, I had an awakening and blew the dust off the journal including entries from 2011 and 2012.

Rather than put these writings in chronological order with the ones written during my hospitalizations in the 1980s, I opted to place them after the earlier musings. In light of the upbeat mood of these writings I feel it would be out of place to have the reader experience them before the darker images in the 1980s.

Candidly, I can tell you that reading these journal entries has given me fresh hope and a new momentum to take my recovery further. As stated several times earlier, I am the only one who can *set myself free!*

Yes, I intend to recapture the joy and giddiness I felt in May 2011 after being properly nourished for a month.

October 21, 1987

Up until today I have only written about my "feelings" after consuming each meal. However, I have come to the realization that further introspection and soul searching are necessary to reap benefit from this experience.

Each day I am amazed at the revelations that occur. Although most of them are painful, I know they won't kill me. If anything, they will stir me into battle.

It would have been easy and right on target had I left here Tuesday before giving myself the last chance to do 100% of all meals and snacks. I am so fearful of failure and rejection that I was going to reject (thus fail) before I could be "ejected." The frustration I felt and coldness from the group were real; however, I gave negative "vibes" and didn't let them into me...not being real, hiding behind a wall of terror and fear at appearing dumb, etc...

Fat and fear of food are so primary in my brain that I often fail to focus on the real issues and this was frustrating to others. They know that fat and food (fear) are not the real issues and they wanted substance to work with. Now that I have opened up more and given support (they realize it isn't easy for me) I feel accepted. I still fear rejection but try harder to block it out.

I've also been making efforts to turn negatives into positives. It isn't easy but it feels good each time I succeed.

The price and terror of giving up my anorexic existence is growing more fierce as I eat each bite. The feelings of fat are colliding with my positive strides and at times I get frightened that I'll never LIVE.

God, please give me the strength and courage to find my way out of this self-made prison which has been my "security." Please help me see and believe that other possibilities exist...possibilities that hold promise and meaning. I do want to LIVE but am so afraid.

Each day I will strive to be more loving to myself—I realize that even the little things count. Thank you for providing me with all of the external support (family, staff, patients and friends) necessary for successful resolution of a life-sapping conflict.

October 22, 1987

Although I am 32 and an adult in many ways, there is still a part of me which has failed to mature...crippling me from living a full and meaningful life...

At one point in my life I believed that food and my anorexic existence were the cause of my failure to develop into an emotionally competent adult. Now, after much pain and introspection, I have come to realize that my self-inflicted starvation and deprivation were my smoke screen used to bury all the "feelings" that were too frightening to deal with.

Perfection, does it exist? I always thought and sometimes fell victim to the notion that I have to be perfect in whatever endeavors I tackle. Realistically I know that no one being is "perfect," yet I punish myself (through starvation and other "atrocities") for not living up to this ideal. If I didn't get an A in a college course, it was as if I failed. Slowly I am learning and <u>believing</u> that I can't be the perfect daughter, sister, friend, aunt, worker etc.—as there is no such thing. In other words, my being is becoming more authentic.

Each day that I am able to interact with the varied groups that comprise this treatment program, a little part of the "perfection ideal" dissipates. I also see that I'm not alone in my struggle—others have tried in vain to reach the impossible dream.

Though I know I'll never be completely "recovered" and that certain aspects of my anorexic mind set will remain, I am striving to say good-bye to the "little girl" inside and hello to the woman who is struggling to emerge and enjoy life.

October 23, 1987

The past 2 days have been almost unbearable. Between the psych testing and other issues which I'm confronting, I really feel as if I'm drowning.

Although I feared I'd do poorly on the intelligence part of the tests, I have a feeling I did average to above average. It's the emotional portion of the tests that stressed me out. The stories that I made up were sad, lonely and dealt with isolation. The parts that touched upon sexuality were the most discomforting. I have finally admitted to myself and others how much I hate my body. I want to be a woman, but I want to be compact and petite.

It has been hard to acknowledge that I'm so filled with negatives. I'm thankful that this has been pointed out and I can try to turn it into positives.

November 5, 1987

Love Means Never Having to Say You're Sorry

Not more than 2 minutes ago I was in a Family Meeting with Dr. C and my parents. Although I got stressed out before and during the meeting, I feel a sense of "numbness" now.

My parents are really trying to understand me and what I need to accomplish so that I can break free from my "prison." However, when they offer support I end up feeling guilty and saying I'm sorry. Even when they tell me I'm more important than their meetings and even bowling, I have a hard time accepting this. Intellectually, I can rationalize and say, "if the tables were turned around," I would give up anything in order to help any family member experiencing difficulty. However, when applied to myself, and I am the recipient rather than the giver, my emotions interfere and the unworthy "mind set" (the sickness) voices itself.

Perhaps I have to begin applying an over-used cliché— Love Means Never Having To Say You're Sorry—to my feelings of unworthiness. Before I can possibly accept the love given by family or others, I am going to have to realize and believe that I am worthwhile. Through self-love I have a chance... a chance to turn my life around. Others can try to help me but if I can't or don't accept help myself, I'll never be able to be <u>REAL</u> and <u>LIVE</u> in a world of <u>FREEDOM</u> and <u>BEAUTY</u>.

November 6, 1987

A Message to Myself

Sometimes I am so busy taking care of and giving to others, that I forget about giving to myself. Hopefully, this "Daily Meditation" I have written for <u>myself</u>, will serve as a reminder that I must treat myself gently and lovingly.

God, thank you for granting me another day to take advantage of life's offerings and the opportunity to work on my goals and dreams.

Though I have not achieved all that I desire, I must not be deterred or fall back.

Each hour of each day, I must remember that my "road to recovery" is a tough one filled with hills, valleys, and crossings.

Please continue to help me believe that I can reach the various destinations I have mapped for myself. Though it won't be easy, I know that I can't successfully complete this journey on my own and pray that I will have the courage to ask for support along the way.

I must continually remember that there are no shortcuts or detours on my "road to recovery." Therefore, I am going to have to exercise <u>patience</u> with every step I take.

If I remember to treat myself to the love and caring that I so freely give to others, my journey will provide me with moments of happiness. These moments can then be used to help me through the "valleys."

Above all, I must remember to love myself...it is only through self-love that my dreams and goals can be reached.

I WILL LIVE MY DREAMS!!!

November 10, 1987

Only If I Eat, Can I Move My Feet

When I begin to obsess about how I feel
I will have to push myself even harder towards
The part of me that really wants to heal.

Rather than run from the "fat"
I must try to discover where my mind is really at.

One way that I can extricate myself from
experiencing defeat
Is to make a promise that only if I eat
Can I move my feet.

Though it won't be easy
And I know I'll feel queasy
I must remember that until I'm well
Too much exercise will surely trigger an alarm bell.

Part of recovering from my illness will be to remember that exercise
will be a reward I have to earn,
Rather than something I engage in to help those calories burn!!!

Dreams Can Come true, I Must Help Them Become Real!!!

November 29, 1987

Although the "authentic" Wailing Wall is located in Israel, I know of a self-created, self-maintained "wailing wall" that travels wherever I go.

Much like a stone or concrete wall, my wall has experienced periods of erosion only to be built up time after time. Often, just when I've felt that I've chiseled an opening that will remain, the cement mixer comes along and obscures my view of the free world.

So, just for the moment, I'm going to let my mind travel beyond the stubborn reality of today into the dreams and hopes of tomorrow.

With the destruction of my wall. I am left without a fortress of defense from the "unknown." Yes, it is frightening, but it is vital to survival.

I'm free as a bird or butterfly and can soar to whatever height I dare. Where will I travel? Undoubtedly I'll travel near and far but no matter where I venture I will go <u>with,</u> rather, than against the flow. I will seek the companionship of others much as a nomad in the desert seeks water.

No longer afraid to be myself, I will take risks and know that even as I may fail, I have learned something from my failure. Being caught up in relationships, self-growth and love will lessen the desire or need to engage in self-destructive behavior.

Breaking down my "Wailing Wall" will allow me to experience life in a new and fulfilling way rather than merely existing.

Through "networking," my dreams of marriage, motherhood, and a satisfying career might become REAL.

My "Wailing Wall" has kept me isolated and "protected" (in an unhealthy way) for so long that I have trouble (or perhaps am afraid) envisioning life beyond.

However, I do know that once I break through, I will be a <u>REAL</u> person…much like Margery Williams' *Velveteen Rabbit* who becomes REAL once he feels loved and accepted.

May 13, 1988

Self Love & Self Respect Will Lead Me To Self Acceptance Which Equals Happiness and More!!!!!!

No one ever said life was going to be easy. However, I feel that my life has been filled with more suffering than joy. Experiencing sadness firsthand has definitely made me an <u>ultra</u>-sensitive and caring person.

Right now, I am facing what will most likely be the hardest task of my life. Living in an anorexic existence for the past 17 years has really narrowed my vision and restricted my boundaries. Because I want to transcend my life of rigidity and control I am trying to believe that others know what is best for me at the present time. Though I am terrified of giving up the <u>unhealthy</u> security of anorexia, I am also afraid not to let it go. I'm at the point where I don't think I can live with it or without it. I must push very hard to believe that there is much life and beauty beyond the confines of my "structured" world.

One thing that I truly like doing is giving to others. Whether that giving takes the form of material things or inspirational guidance, I always feel a sense of happiness when I can impart something good to others.

During this hospitalization for help with my anorexia I am more willing to <u>receive</u> and am trying to help others by sharing some of my pain and joy with them. Though right now I am feeling scared and doubtful, I have told the others that the program does help--- even if you don't feel it immediately---you will feel it when reflecting. It is the taste of life that I have experienced which pushes me on to savor more. Listening to others and their experiences both good and bad, makes me feel more in synch with myself. There is not one person who doesn't experience sadness in his/her existence.

My hope is to "recover" from my anorexic life and then use my experiences—both painful and joyful—to help others avoid some of the hell I have known.

October 16, 1988

Dear "Team,"

This past Thursday I celebrated an anniversary—one year since I first entered your program at Hahnemann.

Since October 13, 1987, I have experienced more of life than in the last 10–15 years put together.

Though I am still traveling the "road to recovery" I am able to live and yes, enjoy things. Before exposure to the program, I was so rigid and set in my ways. You challenged me and now I'm challenging myself.

Yes, I still have many fears and apprehensions about "breaking free," however, I'm determined.

I truly believe that "recovery" is more difficult than starving. It's amazing how things have a different perspective when one isn't constantly obsessing about fat, calories, etc.

As I continue therapy with Dr. Gordon I'm able to realize that life doesn't have to be all or nothing. Hopefully, one day I'll be able to help others as you all have helped me. Again, thanks for the challenge.

God bless you.

Fairwinds Treatment Center

Admission Date: May 2, 2011

Discharge Date: May 31, 2011

May 11, 2011

12:40 p.m.

The more food I am eating, the more anxious I am becoming. While the blueberry muffin during yesterday's snack challenge was delicious, I obsessed about it for a good portion of the day. I kept thinking about what the scale would say this morning. When I couldn't eat dinner last night because I was too full from the large apple that was given to me at snack, I felt like a failure. Black and white thinking in action. The happiness I felt about successfully meeting snack challenge was negated and I felt awful even though I matched the caloric content by consuming a Boost supplement.

I wasn't too freaked out when the scale was up by ¼ of a pound this morning. What really upset me is when I saw what was laid out for my breakfast. Since I knew that my caloric total was rising to 1100, I figured I'd get an ounce extra here or a double portion of peanut butter. When there were two packages of oatmeal (one more than usual—100 calories) and ¾ cup cottage cheese vs. ½ cup and one cup cantaloupe vs. 1/2, I was angry and frustrated. Though I wanted to check things out with the group, I felt that other people's issues were more important than mine so I withheld until after my session with Dr. Berkus (Director of the program at Fairwinds). She told me to "put the yardstick" away and use the group as a resource for recovery. It was uncomfortable returning to Susan's group and opening myself up. As difficult as it is, I have to remember that questioning my beliefs through self-exposure is the only way out of my self-created prison. I want to do it, I must do it, I CAN DO IT!

May 12, 2011

8:30 p.m.

Tonight I'm feeling anxious because the scale went up a pound and tomorrow my calories will be increased to 1200. When I found out that we weren't required to finish the whole personal pizza we had the option of making for lunch, I was disappointed that I didn't at least try it.

In an effort to make sure I select a variety and choices I normally wouldn't for next week's menu planning, I got a jump start on it today. Now I'm not sure if this is a good thing or if it falls under obsessing. I will try the frozen yogurt, pancakes and French toast. If it's true that a calorie is a calorie, then it shouldn't matter whether I have an apple or something I might enjoy more. I need to push myself to diversify my menu. No more dry tuna!

I'm finding it difficult to express myself through the art therapy assignments. Though I consider myself to be creative, when it comes to drawing my feelings, it is a bit far out. Why do I feel so much fatter if I've only gained a pound? I'm also freaking out because it's been 1 ½ weeks since I have done Pilates. I am trying to be less focused on food, calories and fat but am finding it difficult. I Will; I WANT, I CHOOSE and I DESIRE.

May 14, 2011

9:35 a.m.

I'm feeling as if I have won the lottery—yesterday I consumed 1300 calories and even had a piece of hard candy last night and this morning the scale was down ¾ of a pound. Yes, I know it is not my goal to lose weight here but I can't help but be happy, no, make that elated that I can really eat and not have my weight go out of control. I can't even begin to think of the wonderful possibilities which may await me in a life without restricting and starving. I guess my true test is next week when I eat the doughnut, macaroni and cheese and stuffed shells. Wouldn't it be wonderful if I could have a normal portion of these foods without gaining weight? Who knows, maybe the glucophage and synthroid I am taking for my hyperinsulinemia is what is keeping my body in balance. All I know is I am truly happy…something I haven't been for a long time.

While I'm happy about the food stuff, I feel like I'm being strangled inside. Yesterday, when I walked into Michael's and saw the stuff for Father's Day, I fell apart. God only knows how much I loved and still love my daddio and how much I miss him. I truly believe that the greatest gift I could give to him is to break free from the anorexia and enjoy a real life. I want to believe that my dad is still with me and is aware how I am trying to break free. Although I know I can't go back in time, I wish I had the opportunity to spend quality time with my beloved dad free from the anorexia. Daddy, I love you very much— more than all the stars in the sky; grains of sand on the beach and stars in the sky combined. You are my hero forever and always.

May 16, 2011

10:30 p.m.

As the day wore on my fear and anxiety about food increased. I'm not sure if it's because I tried several new things—chicken tortilla soup at lunch, veggie burger with cheese in a spinach wrap for dinner followed by frozen yogurt with 2 TBS of mini chocolate chips for evening snack.

I'm still very anxious about gaining weight and am feeling fatter and fatter. Every morning and night I check to see if I can still see my rib cage and make sure my pelvic bones are still visible. This is so sick and I want to stop. I really want to eat normally and not be fat. How am I ever going to get comfortable with my body? Not having done my Pilates routine for the past two weeks is also not helping my body image. I am grateful that I can walk for 20 minutes a day

Seeing the new patient who was admitted late in the day freaked me out. I have never seen a person so thin and pitiful looking. I thank God that I never got to that point. (Note, she was deemed too ill to be treated at Fairwinds and was discharged to a hospital for treatment.)

I hope I can summon the strength and courage to break free to enjoy life. Although I will never be 100% free and able to view food as just food, I need and want to be able to give up its control of my existence. I am determined and believe that the staff at Fairwinds knows what they are doing. Wendy, now is the time for you to move forward. YOU CAN DO IT!!!

May 18, 2011

9:30 a.m.

Oh, how bloated and fat I feel. This morning I did not have to be weighed and not knowing the number is anxiety producing. I'm not sure if it would have been better to get weighed backwards because I'm thinking what "if" I gained too much because of the doughnut, etc. I realize this is irrational but these are my feelings.

The feelings of insecurity about not knowing my weight reminds me of how as a child at Camp JCC during swimming lessons I would not go into the pond if I couldn't hold onto the bottom. Well, dear Wendy, the time has come to let go and dive in. Your life (at least the quality of it), depends upon your ability to free yourself of <u>ALL</u> the trappings of the anorexia. YOU CAN DO IT!

May 19, 2011

I am overjoyed beyond belief that despite eating 1400 calories yesterday, my weight was ___ this morning. [*I am intentionally omitting the weight in these entries as I know it could act as a trigger for those afflicted with anorexia nervosa.*] While I realize I shouldn't be focusing on a number and that inevitably I will most likely gain a few pounds, I am thrilled it appears I no longer have to restrict and starve. In fact, I'd be afraid to go back to starving for fear that my metabolism would really go haywire. Yesterday, being told that I have osteopenia was a smack of reality. Though at age 56 I might have had bone loss anyhow, I can't help but believe the reason I have it now (still fairly young—I think, hope ☺) is because of all my years of restricting and starving. I deserve better and will play an active part in making sure I get what I need and want. I still can't believe I am eating normally and the scale has not betrayed me. I am woman and I will SOAR!

May 22, 2011

4:25 p.m.

What a wonderful day I've had. After finding my way to Mandi's bridal shower (I was out on a pass), the real challenge began. Most of the other guests had already arrived and I made a beeline for Mali who was happy to see me.

There was a wide selection of food to choose from: assorted bagels, lox, cream cheese, tomatoes, salad, tuna salad, egg salad, blintze soufflé, quiche (crustless), kugel, pastries, nuts with Craisins and a fruit salad. Before I left Fairwinds I was told that my calorie count for lunch was 700—when I heard the number I flinched but was determined to do the best I could. I took a plate (by the way I had my 10:00 a.m. snack of Fiber One cereal and 4 oz. of skim Lactaid at home—in fact, I asked for the snack before I left) and put a bit of salad (including candied pecans), two tomato slices, ½ bakery cinnamon raisin bagel, 1 TBS tuna salad, miniscule amount of blintz soufflé, and a tiny portion of quiche on it. Unfortunately, when I got to the table, Pam had already put my drink (diet coke) at a place other than next to Mali. I truthfully intended to eat only ¼ of the half of bagel and then I thought about how well I have been doing and why would I want to blow it. Besides, I thought, I was supposed to have 700 calories for lunch.

It was a struggle and my hands were shaking but I <u>ate everything</u> I had put on my plate! No, eating the pastries for dessert was out of the question so I took a few pieces of cantaloupe, one blackberry, a few blueberries, one little piece of watermelon, three almonds, one Craisin, and one pistachio nut and I ate all of it!!! I felt bloated but content and proud of myself. I knew I fell short of the 700 calorie goal but to me what I accomplished was amazing.

When I came back to Fairwinds and said that I had between 350 and 500 calories, so I would eat something extra for dinner, I was HAPPY to find out that Jean had given me the wrong number. I only needed to eat 500 calories for lunch. Victory tastes sweet and so did the food, especially the pecans!!!

May 25, 2011

Anxious, stressed, and unsure are the words which best describe my feelings today. After confirming my discharge date is next Tuesday, May 31 I am beginning to get "stage fright." As difficult as it has been to eat and follow the program while here, I suspect it will be harder when I am on my own. However, I have to look at the "big picture" and remember how unhappy I was when starving and restricting. When I leave here I will do my best to continue having three meals and three snacks daily. I will be open to trying new things and hopefully as my life becomes full I will place less focus on calories, the scale and how fat I feel.

My feelings of sadness over dad's not being here to witness the transformation which is taking place in his "Wendellah" is understandable. However, Dr. Berkus and Mali believe he does know what is going on. Mom thinks dad is my guardian angel who orchestrated this whole scene and yesterday Mali reminded me about the very first week of Intensive Outpatient treatment (IOP) when a guy named George (my late dad's name) came to the group and then stopped coming because he didn't think it was for him. God, how I want to believe that my beloved dad is with me on my journey to recovery. Dad, thank you for being the most wonderful father a girl could have. I hope you know how proud I am to be your daughter.

May 26, 2011

STRESSED OUT! To have the scale go up to ___ today felt like a hard kick in the teeth. I am so afraid that between now and discharge on Tuesday, May 31 my weight is going to be like a runaway train. Adding fuel to the fire is that last Friday when we did menu planning, I went way outside my comfort zone and ordered veggie lasagna for dinner tonight. Early this morning I asked Kourtney (the nutritionist) if I could change my dinner selection and she said no. Although I understand why I can't, I am still frustrated, nervous and upset.

Going out to lunch at the pizza place today was overwhelming and I almost started to cry. Ordering pizza and a salad was hard to do; especially when I saw the prices! It didn't matter that I wasn't paying, it was just uncomfortable to spend $2.50 on additional toppings plus a salad for $3.99 and Diet Pepsi for $1.99. It was also stressful when the drinks came and all of the "Diet Pepsi's" had a lemon wedge on the glass except for Kristin and myself. I immediately got scared the waiter gave me regular Pepsi and was distressed. At first I think Kourtney and Susan (a therapist) thought I was being ridiculous but then they both agreed I could/should ask the waitress about it. When I inquired and apologized, she said it's ok, maybe she gave me regular Pepsi and she suggested she take the glass in front of me and get a new one she would "pour." Yes, I felt a bit dumb and even doubted if she really changed out the contents in the glass but in the end I drank the drink, ate the salad and had an entire slice of pizza. The whole time I kept thinking about oh no, I still have to eat three more times today.

I wish I could have been relaxed and have enjoyed the people and conversation around me during lunch than to be focused on what the calories might do to me and how fat I feel.

May 27, 2011

The tension is mounting. Meal planning for next week seemed like a monumental task. Although I know I need and want to continue with the program on my own, I am truly doubtful of how I can do it. Planning a menu, shopping and cooking seems like a tall order for someone "just starting out." Although I planned my menu, I can envision myself "substituting" items. This will not necessarily be bad as long as I match them calorie for calorie. It is unrealistic to expect that I will be able to have ALL of my meals and snacks at the exact time I had them at Fairwinds. It's almost like a juggling act. I have come so far and do not want to lose ground. "God, <u>please</u> grant me the serenity to accept the things I cannot change, courage to change the things I can and wisdom to know the difference." I CAN AND WILL DO THIS, my life depends on it!

Hey Wendy, what do you think about eating pizza and pasta in the same day and having the scale remain the same? Interesting! Maybe it is time to really ease up on the reins.

4:35 p.m.

What a brave thing to do—I chose not to go on the outing to the beach and was able to finish up some art projects. Several others also stayed behind. At 3:00 p.m. I expected Donna to herd us into the cafeteria for snack. When the clock said 3:25 and we still hadn't been given our 3:00 p.m. snack I thought about just forgetting it and also the consequences if staff later realized the mistake that was made. So I hesitantly asked Donna when we were going to have snack and she was embarrassed that she had completely forgotten about it. I was sure the others would be mad at me for speaking up. Rather, one of them praised me for being honest.

May 28, 2011

9:55 p.m.

What a great day it was. After leaving Fairwinds I went to the post office to pick up my mail and request they begin delivering it on Tuesday, May 31. It was an impressive stack. As I got out of the car and walked to the post office I saw an elderly veteran standing in the doorway selling poppies (yes, it is Memorial Day weekend). I immediately thought of my beloved dad (also a veteran) and decided I'd buy poppies on my way out. For some reason I changed my mind and bought a poppy for me and one for mom before going in. I told the guy that my dad was a WWII veteran who passed away this past October. I thanked the man for his service to our country and three minutes later when I came out of the post office he was no longer there.

Who would ever have believed that I would sit in Subway with Mali and share a package of cheddar Sun Chips. I truly feel as if I am a new person. There is no way I can ever go back to the life I led before entering Fairwinds. All I can say tonight is I truly believe I have a chance at enjoying a productive and happy life. Mom, thank you for your support and encouragement and dad thank you for always being there. I love you both dearly.

May 29, 2011

Another great day! After breakfast I took a 35-minute walk, went to community meeting, showered and had snack. I was pleased that although I failed to order milk with my 10:00 a.m. Fiber One cereal, I decided to go to the refrigerator in the canteen to get skim Lactaid. On the way home to my apartment when I discovered I had forgotten to take my afternoon snack, I got anxious and realized I could buy something at the grocery store. I bought a Weight Watchers macaroni and cheese dinner and a box of Rice Krispie treats. The macaroni and cheese was good but I didn't feel satisfied after eating. I think I either needed more to drink or should have added a veggie or fruit. Had a Rice Krispie treat at 3:00 p.m. and still felt hungry.

Mom and I went to the Outback and I ordered the kid's chicken with steamed veggies and a baked sweet potato which I shared with mom. Still felt hungry and embarrassed for feeling so. After I dropped mom off I had a dialogue with myself and ended up stopping at the market to buy an apple to eat. My reward for "listening" to my body was a wonderfully crisp and sweet Pink Lady apple!!! I felt "guilty" but enjoyed the apple as I drove back to my apartment to pick up some Miralax before returning to Fairwinds. I was looking forward to my ½ cup of frozen yogurt, 1 TBS chocolate chips and graham crackers tonight and was majorly disappointed when there was nothing prepared for me. Since the kitchen was closed, I opted to have the top of a bran muffin—it was very good! I am proud of myself for "winging it" and listening to my body. I am convinced there is no way I will ever go back to starving myself again.

June 1, 2011

11:30 p.m.

Day one of being home from my month's stay at Fairwinds Treatment Center was a challenge but I am proud I did what I was supposed to do. I may have short-changed myself a little (no more than 100 or 200 calories) as I'm relying on Kourtney's directive to go by number of servings per food group rather than calories.

It was an effort and it took a lot of self-talk to get out of bed at 7:45 a.m. to eat breakfast. Then I truly surprised myself at 10:15 a.m. when I allowed myself to have ½ a mini panetone I bought last December (1/2 half is equal to two grains). Sitting down to eat it with a cup of coffee was a real treat. Lunch did not seem overwhelming but I had to do a lot of self-talk to eat the whole apple for afternoon snack.

Returning to IOP and not knowing anyone was difficult as I felt like an outsider. Having to select my dinner for tonight and tomorrow put me in a bit of a tizzy. Although I wanted to try the manicotti the voice of ED (eating disorder) won over and I played it safe with a veggie burger and ½ a spinach wrap. However, to get up to my protein shares, I threw some chick peas into my salad and had two TBS of shredded cheese on my veggie burger. Yes, I did get hungry and thought about delaying meals and snacks but then remembered how good it feels to have fuel. I am so proud of myself for walking two miles tonight (even more proud I opted out of Pilates last night because my a.m. walk and the emotional aspects of leaving Fairwinds had wiped me out).

Spending one hour in the grocery store to purchase several items was not ideal but I have to cut myself some slack. To have gone from inpatient where all my meals were plated for the past month to suddenly purchasing, preparing and then eating the food is a tall order. Hopefully, as I become more comfort able with my choices and continue to see that my weight stays pretty much the same consuming approximately 1500 calories I will find things easier to navigate. In the meantime I will keep pushing myself to continue along the path I started at Fairwinds.

June 7, 2011

1:15 p.m.

Today is one week since I've been discharged from Fairwinds and I can't believe how fantastic I feel! Of course the fact that the scale says ___ also plays into the equation of how happy I am. Never before in my life have I had this much energy or enthusiasm for life. I am getting positive feedback from everyone who sees me. Despite the fact that I only gained one pound while at Fairwinds, people are telling me how great I look. On Saturday at shul someone asked me if I had Botox. I said no, are you crazy? Her response was you look 10 years younger and your wrinkles are gone. I said I didn't have wrinkles to which she responded, yes you did!

Even my dear friend Mali and I have gotten "closer" if that is possible. Now that I am willing and able to eat "normally," we can have a friendship on a different level. (Previously, she would lecture me on the cons of restricting, etc.) I truthfully never thought about how my anorexia affected my family and friends. Being told that it was difficult to include me in dinner plans because she felt uncomfortable eating when I wasn't was kind of "eye opening." Yes, I am still caught up in the anorexic mindset and God forbid if I gain an ounce. However, I am hopeful that as I work through the demons, I will find a way to let go of the behaviors which have put my life on hold for so long.

At age 56 I am beginning to enjoy the little pleasures in life most people don't even think about. This past Sunday when I met Anne Meyer at Panera and ate ½ tuna sandwich on a whole grain baguette was amazing. I almost cried at how overwhelmed I was at completing such a simple and "normal" act. I need to keep my focus on what I truly want and deserve from life. The best way I can respect and pay homage to my beloved dad is to embrace life and continue to do acts of loving kindness in his honor. Mom has been a great source of support and it is wonderful to see her so upbeat. No matter how tired I may be I have to push myself to write in this journal daily. Life is wonderful and I am happy to be alive!

June 10, 2011

10:32 p.m.

Yesterday was a bad day all around. When the scale said ___ I felt upset, let down and unsure. As difficult as it was, I followed the "plan" and this morning I smiled and breathed a "sigh of relief" when it said ___. I hope as time goes on I will be able to accept slight increases in the scale without letting it color my whole day. The fact that yesterday was eight months since my dear dad died and I went to Shavuot Yizkor services (a special memorial service) did not help either. One day at a time. "God grant me the serenity to accept the things I cannot change, courage to change the things I can and wisdom to know the difference."

June 12, 2011

2:38 p.m.

I'm happy and sad at the same time. Happy I was able to go to Anna and Will's B'nai Mitzvah yesterday and eat at the luncheon (1 to 2 oz. salmon, salad, mini spinach pie and cocktail eggplant lasagna) and then have the scale be down this morning. Sad because it is clear that the damn scale and its numbers still rule my life. It's great to be eating, feeling good and socializing but I do hope at some point to be able to give up the scale.

After I finish this entry I am going to pick mom up and head for Mandi and Michael's wedding. I am looking forward to sharing this simcha (happy event) with my mutually adoptive family and being present in every sense of the word. Go girl GO! Thank you Fairwinds, I love you ALL!!

Fairwinds Treatment Center

Admission Date: Aug. 15, 2011

Discharge Date: Sept. 13, 2011

August 16, 2011

Wow, I just finished reading entries from several months ago and can't believe what I wrote. I was really feeling "on top of the world" and had confidence things would get better! What happened? I think my setback is a combination of the antidepressant shutting down a bit combined with my gradual lessening of caloric intake. By now I should be "smart enough" to realize that food is necessary for healthy functioning.

What struck me the most as I read my journaling from May and June is how I kept on harping about the number on the scale. Although I'm anxious about it, especially since I'm now on Abilify (an antidepressant with weight gain as a side effect), I think it's best that I not see or know what direction the scale is moving in.

Last night it was difficult but I am proud of myself for giving my scale to Dr. Alan Feldman (my psychiatrist). Yes, I have gotten rid of scales in the past only to replace them. However, this time I truly feel different. I realize that for me there is no such thing as having "a little bit of scale." Not when the number dictates the quality of my life.

I am hoping and praying that this period of partial hospitalization will get me back on track. Ultimately, it is <u>ME</u> who is responsible for what choices I make. Now that I have had the opportunity to feel totally alive and enjoy life, I prefer that to living life on the sidelines. It's funny because several months ago I wrote about how the quality of Mali's and my friendship had changed. Sadly, we're back to the "old" dance where she is lecturing me about how my restricting food is hurting my quality of life. I need to get a grip on myself and despite the feelings of fatness, etc. keep moving forward. When push comes to shove, in the final analysis, will it really matter if I am a size 2, 4, 6, or 8? Probably not.

As long as I nourish myself properly and exercise within normal limits, I should be okay. I need to remember that I am 56 not 16 and my body cannot withstand the abuse without consequences for much longer. "God grant me the serenity to accept the things I cannot change, courage to change the things I can, and the wisdom to know the difference."

August 18, 2011

Happy Birthday dear daddy—I love you and miss you and promise to give my total self to recovery.

Can you imagine what my life could be like if I weren't strangled by the depression and anorexia? Thanks to you and mom I have the education, ability and desire to make something worthwhile out of my life. Right now I'm still in jail but I am the only person who has the power to release me—"the jailor with the keys."

Yes, life without the anorexia would be totally different but different can be good. Based upon how I felt when I left here in May, different can be fantastic. I promise to be mindful of what I am doing or saying that may impede my desire to grow and recover. No, I am not stupid and don't know why I continuously call myself stupid. Anyone who can polish off a crossword puzzle as I do, is not stupid. Dad, you know how much I miss you and today I will try even harder to live the kind of life that would make you happy and proud. I can DO THIS and I WILL DO THIS!

August 21, 2011

I can't remember feeling this full. It's as if I ate several Thanksgiving dinners! Truthfully, breakfast was totally satisfying and filling. Had I been left to my own devices, I probably wouldn't have had a major meal for lunch such as I did here. The feelings of fat are becoming more intense and I keep thinking the other patients and staff are wondering what in hell I am doing here because I look like a cow. After talking to Kourtney, the tech, I understand if I am feeling this full at dinner time it may be easier to supplement.

Guess my stomach is really not used to having the quantity of food I am now consuming and perhaps when planning my menu I need to choose some foods which are more calorie dense. I'm a little afraid of getting used to eating so much and then I won't be able to stop. It's kind of sad because my mood seems a bit brighter but the fear of calories and weight is still dominant in my mind.

August 27, 2011

Letter to my body: An assignment from
Susan, the therapist

Dear Wendy's Body,

First, I apologize for all the abuse I have put you through over the years. At the age of 56 I now look back and shudder when I think about some of the things I did to you, all in the name of looking good.

I am hopeful and need to believe that my time at Fairwinds is truly going to be what it takes to make me change my cruel ways. Restricting food, fluids and then over exercising would not be acceptable in a prison setting, yet I have lived my life in such a manner for many years.

Until my inpatient stay at Fairwinds this past spring, I had no idea how horrible I felt. After one month of good nutrition and balanced exercise I had more energy and vitality than ever before. I had proof positive that food = good mood. However, the anorexia spoke louder than good feelings and I soon followed its lead rather than being led by wisdom.

I am no longer youthful and do not have my whole life in front of me. It is entirely up to me to begin respecting and worshipping my body. No longer can I push you to the limits I have. As I've said before, I am the jailor with the keys to my own prison.

When I am better nourished I am happier and better able to cope with whatever life dishes out. I may struggle but chances are I won't sink if I am truly taking care of my body.

Now is the time to LET GO of the eating disorder and welcome myself as a 56-year-old woman who wants happiness and success from life. If I eat, play, work and study in good measure, the future can be mine.

August 29, 2011

Having "extra" time at home last night was worthwhile. Although I am still tired I feel more rested. This morning as I was getting dressed and fixing my hair I actually spoke out loud to myself declaring that I AM NOT FAT. I figure if I keep saying this then maybe eventually I will believe it. Again, as anxious as I'm feeling not weighing myself and seeing the number every day, I think it's for the best. Keeping in mind that I was told I weigh less than ___ really calmed me to the point where I am considering just "meeting" in the middle and saying as long as I can eat and weigh between ___ and ___ I can live with it. While I may never truly see myself as I am, I can't discount how much better I feel when my mind and body are nourished.

September 5, 2011

Congratulations Wendy! Saturday night was a challenge but you did it! I can't believe how worked up I got about meeting Mali and Fred for dinner. My head really hurt and when I called to cancel the date I wasn't prepared for Mali to say wait until later. As I thought about things I realized that while my head did hurt, I was reverting to "ancient" behavior of when I used a phantom ailment to get out of a social situation. As difficult as it was (I was shaking when I drove to meet them), I met Mali and Fred and we had a great time! I was hungry and eating with them was not such a big issue—go figure. The real challenge was when Mandi called and asked if we wanted to meet her and Mike at Dairy Queen. OK, how could I just sit there while everyone else ate. So, after looking at the nutritional information (not that abnormal), I ordered a kid sized vanilla dish dipped in chocolate. OMG—this was delicious. I was the last one done eating but I ate and enjoyed the whole thing and have decided to visit DQ once a month. If a calorie is a calorie, then 200 calories spent on DQ is ok in my book!

September 6, 2011

Last night I felt panicked when I was still so hungry at the end of the day. I thought perhaps I had gone out of my weight range and Kourtney decreased my caloric intake. When I got home I ate two stalks of celery, one TBS low-fat cream cheese and ½ cup Fiber One cereal (before snack) and was still hungry. In speaking with Kourtney this morning she suggested maybe I was hungry because of a small deficit on Sunday or perhaps I'm not drinking enough. It's ok to feel hungry and eat a little more in a controlled way. Wendy, your clothes still fit and that is a good thing. Please ease up on yourself—it's not worth going crazy over.

October 18, 2011

Wow, it's been a long time since I have written anything. Well, the past few weeks have been rocky but things are beginning to settle down. Dr. Feldman has been so kind and patient with me. Last Friday when he told me I needed to <u>really</u> <u>structure</u> my days, he was right on! Since last Saturday I have gotten out of the house everyday and am feeling brighter. I now see how getting out can help improve my mood and outlook.

Although missing breakfast yesterday was not totally my fault (had to leave at 5:20 a.m. to take mom for her colonoscopy), I do see how missing a meal can throw me way off. Even though I tried to make up for the lost breakfast I couldn't. At 5:15 a.m. I had a TBS of peanut butter; at 8:30 a.m. a Fiber One bar; at noon a cheese sandwich and an apple; at 3:20 four cups of popcorn and 4 oz. Boost and at 4:30 p.m. I had ½ cup Fiber One cereal and rode my bike four miles and did Pilates. I was starved and went out to buy an already prepared chicken. Had six oz. with cooked veggies and a slice of bread. For snack I had a Weight Watchers ice cream bar and at 9:30 p.m. I "pigged out" on ½ cup frozen yogurt and 1 TBS peanut butter. I felt scared and annoyed as I hit 1700 calories. This was the first time I ever ate my "optional" calories.

Today I have followed a regular food plan and feel much better. It's amazing how a meal or snack can make such a huge difference. No, it's not easy by any means but I think I'm on the right track! :)

Fairwinds Treatment Center

Admission Date: Feb. 3, 2012

Discharge Date: Feb. 17, 2012

February 4, 2012

Wow, I just read my entry from October 18, 2011 and kind of wish I had read it a lot sooner. In recent weeks I have been cutting back on snacks, portion size, etc. Although to my knowledge I haven't lost weight, my mood is poor. My anxiety got worse a few weeks ago when I bought a scale and saw that I weighed ___ (the most I have been in several years). Since then I seem to have slacked off— something I can't afford to do as food definitely affects my mood. I'm feeling fatter and more self-conscious about my appearance.

Because of my increased anxiety, Dr. Feldman prescribed Buspar— proved to be a huge mistake. I ended up in a locked psychiatric unit at Memorial Hospital in Tampa and I was freaked out. For two days I ate about 500 to 600 calories and this added to my depression. It was suggested that I return to Fairwinds and I said no.

Once I got home, Beth from admissions at Fairwinds called and I agreed to come back for two weeks (my third time there) for some fine tuning. It's very hard being here at a "normal" weight. I feel as if I shouldn't be here. However, in my heart, I know that ED still has a hold on me even though the scale is not down. That's probably the hardest thing about ED— being "sick" and not looking the part.

I agreed to an ECT consult as I believe my down mood is keeping me stuck. Yet, I'm down for valid reasons but maybe as Dr. Berkus said, "a jump start" could be what I need to get going. I'll be honest and listen to what the doctor says and then make up my mind. I'm tired of feeling down and would like to see the bright side again.

February 5, 2012

Even though I have been eating appropriately for the past few days my mood is still down. I don't feel motivated to do much of anything.

Eating the pasta and Alfredo sauce was difficult; especially because the sauce was in a separate bowl. I thought the sauce was also going to be a chicken sauce and was totally blindsided by the actual meal. To get through it I reminded myself that at home I occasionally allow myself a Lean Cuisine macaroni and cheese dinner—pasta in a different form. Do I like chicken Alfredo? I wouldn't go out of my way to eat it again.

I'm nervous about the thought of an ECT consult. While it seems brutal, I also want to feel better and get on with my life. Perhaps if I felt better I'd be able to add more things to my life. Don't know what's going on—where's the chicken, where's the egg— I'm feeling stuck in a revolving door.

February 7, 2012

I don't want to "jinx" myself but I think the fog has lifted a little. I feel a little more comfortable with the other people and will try harder to participate in group sessions today. I feel fat and am worried about where I am on the scale but of most concern is my down mood. While some of it is definitely due to several days of minimal nutrition, I believe that a portion of it is chemical. This is the first time in my life I am entertaining the idea of just "dealing with the number" as long as my mood is stabilized. I'm tired of being depressed. If my weight remains in the "normal" range, I have no reason to feel badly as far as this is concerned. I'm almost 57 and wish as I might and try as hard as possible, my body is not going to look the way I would like it to.

I'm not sure about ECT and hope I can get a consult soon so I know what my options are.

February 8, 2012

Today is the best I've felt in awhile. Yes, I believe there is a direct correlation to the fact that I am eating a balanced meal plan. If only I can find the way to continue to do so when left to my own devices. I have to be more vigilant regarding snacks. There really is no middle ground when you come down to it. Missing cumulative snacks and medication does have a way of letting ED gain control.

No, I'm not thrilled with how I look but in reality I know I don't look as bad as I see myself. For once and ever, Wendy, now is the time to move forward and embrace a happy and healthy life which can be yours. Except for me, no one really cares what the number on the scale says or what size dress or pants I am wearing. Somehow I have to find peace in my own body and accept that I will never be satisfied with my looks. God knows I am not a shallow person who judges others by their looks, so why should I be so hard on myself?

In some ways this stay at Fairwinds is like a refresher course reminding me of what I want and how to get it. Hopefully, when I walk away this time I will continue to implement the tools I have learned. I need to be willing to let go of hiding beneath shawls and eating the same menu over and over. Remember, variety is the spice of life. Others have overcome the obstacles and pitfalls of anorexia so why shouldn't I? Wendy, you are the jailor with the keys and only you can throw them away—the sooner the better.

February 10, 2012

A week of eating properly has elevated my spirits but I still feel "off." Yesterday I stayed hydrated <u>ALL</u> day and I'm wondering if I continue to eat and "drink" if I will feel that much better. I think I will ask for privileges during contract negotiation meeting. Walking 15 minutes in the parking lot is better than nothing!

I know it will be challenging and difficult when I leave here but I have to continue eating my meals and snacks within 1500 calories. It is so true that relapses begin by skipping one snack multiplied by many.

I am grateful mom is ok and is so supportive in my attempt to recover. She is a good woman and deserves to have a daughter she doesn't have to worry about.

A "Little Help From My Friends"

Toby

No matter how strong a person may be, there is no way on earth that they can deal with and survive an eating disorder without assistance from others. In addition to my loving parents George and Beverly Levine, brother Barry, and many health care professionals along the way, I owe a debt of gratitude to several people who stood by me as I tried to extricate myself from the chains of anorexia nervosa. Although some "friends" decided that they were too "afraid" of losing me to the disorder and jumped ship in order to save themselves the pain, one friend in particular stood by me since our first encounter which indeed made us friends.

Toby Lempert Bleeck, now a wife, mother, nurse and always a FRIEND, is truly an anchor in my life. Our friendship began some 35 years ago on New Year's Eve in Boston at a mutual friend's party. Although neither of us has maintained contact with this other friend, Toby and I have created a friendship which surpasses all time and physical distance.

As two single women in Boston, we spent a fair amount of time engaged in the hunt for the perfect man. Aside from attending various singles activities only to walk away with our friendship, we shared our feelings, hopes, and fears with one another. When I met Toby, she was transitioning from her career as a teacher to that of a registered nurse. I was working at Blue Cross Blue Shield of Massachusetts in downtown Boston. Between our work schedules and Toby's studying, we managed to have "fun" in the big city. Whether it was idly passing a weekend afternoon people-watching at Boston's Quincy Marketplace, or meandering around Coolidge Corner in Brookline, Massachusetts, we always managed to keep abreast of one another's trials and tribulations of the previous week.

When I first met Toby, my anorexia had not "officially" been diagnosed (i.e. I struggled with food and weight issues without looking overtly anorexic). At some point in our relationship the anorexia was diagnosed, and I began therapy. In retrospect, I imagine it was not easy for anyone who knew me to watch as I gradually began to disappear. While some friends bowed out, Toby provided support, encouragement, and unconditional love. I remember a particularly bad stretch when my weight had dropped to the low 90s and I was being threatened with hospitalization. The threat coupled with severe depression was enough to leave me unable to do much else except work Monday through Friday and recuperate on the weekends. On weekends when Toby didn't have to work a night shift and had the day free, we would often do something low-key. During the times that she worked or had studying to attend to, I stayed in my apartment. At some point I began taking my phone off the receiver for days at a time so that I would not have to deal with anything. Imagine the verbal beating (prompted by their love for me) that I took from my family. On one occasion I remember Toby was working and I was in my hibernation mode with the phone disconnected. All of a sudden the doorbell rang and rang and rang… After what seemed like forever, I ventured downstairs to see what was causing the bell to consistently ring, only to find Toby poised against the bell. It so happened that she had worked a double shift and tried calling me several times only to get a busy signal. As tired as she was, she would not go home until she checked on me and chided me (rightfully so) for once again taking my phone off the hook.

Anorexia brings with it many strange actions and rituals. Whether it be cutting one's food a certain way or eating at a precise time using specific utensils, the oddities can be tiring and presumably annoying to all involved. Never once did Toby shy away from going anywhere with me as I engaged in all the anorexic fussings. If I declared that I could join her in such-and-such activity but had to be home to prepare something to eat, she got me home on time.

Although I felt as if I was losing my best friend when Toby moved from Boston to New York to marry Norman, Toby and I still keep in touch and recall the old days with bittersweet memories. In fact, when she, Norman, and their two daughters Devorah and Danielle made a visit to my home in Florida during April of 2002, we cooed and squealed so much that our husbands and the girls looked at us and kind of just rolled their eyes. Toby explained to the girls that mommy and Wendy knew each other many years ago...almost a different lifetime.

Mali

Moving from Massachusetts to Florida as a newlywed in January of 2001 was a life-changing event. Having left behind family and friends, I was charged with the task of cultivating new friendships in a different part of the country.

As chance would have it, at the end of my second week as a resident of the "Sunshine State," my path crossed with that of a wonderful woman named Mali Schantz-Feld. From the moment we met, there was a strong connection between us. The fact that we were in the same age range and were both writers further cemented our bond.

Much like Toby, Mali has been a true and trusted friend and we consider one another "sisters." From day one I confided in Mali and she shared with me.

A Chance at Love

For far too many years my eating disorder controlled my life. From missed social opportunities to the scholarship of a lifetime, I sacrificed many years of my existence to a "friend" called anorexia nervosa.

When I hit age 40 the reality sank in that unless I did something drastic, I would most likely spend the rest of my life alone in my studio apartment in Brighton, Massachusetts.

A turning point came after surgery for fibroid tumors when I developed a severe wound infection that necessitated two daily visits by a visiting nurse. Although my poor nutrition did not cause the infection, I knew that it wasn't aiding me in the healing process. During my convalescence I had a lot of time to think and promised God and myself that if I got better, I would try harder to take care of myself.

In addition to voluntarily checking myself into a day treatment program, I began to think about what life might be like if I allowed myself the chance to "take a chance" and live. I was tired of hearing friends and family tell me that no one was going to come knocking on my door. If I wanted to meet people, especially a nice guy, I would have to go out and find him.

Much to my surprise and the shock of those who know me, I wrote a personal ad and placed it in the *Jewish Advocate*, a paper published in Boston for the Jewish community. Because I have always taken pride in my Jewish heritage and identity, I was only interested in dating Jewish men. Besides, I felt it was safer to place an ad in a smaller paper like the *Jewish Advocate* than a larger one such as the *Boston Globe*.

To my surprise, several men responded to my ad. With much apprehension I returned the call I received from a man named

"Geoffrey." I liked the sound of his voice and figured I placed the ad, I might as well give it a shot. During my initial conversation with "Geoff," I learned that he was "a mathematician playing engineer" for a major defense contractor. I also found out that he had been married for 28 ½ years when his beloved wife succumbed to breast cancer after a prolonged battle. Geoff worked in Massachusetts but lived in New Hampshire with his 21-year-old son. With our phone conversation almost at a close, we agreed to meet for dinner at the Cheesecake Factory the following Friday evening in Chestnut Hill, Massachusetts.

At this juncture in my life, going out to dinner was not something that I looked forward to. Although I was at a "low normal" weight, I preferred the "safety" of eating what I had prepared. However, I had made a promise to myself and God and I was going to try. Geoff and I were both anxious about making a good impression that I don't think he noticed that I "played" with my four-cheese angel hair pasta. Whew! With dinner over we headed to a nearby synagogue to attend Sabbath services. The evening ended fairly early and when Geoff dropped me off at my apartment before heading back to New Hampshire, I thanked him for the evening and wished him a safe drive. Based on how I perceived the evening went, I did not expect to hear from him again.

The following Monday I was shocked and pleased to receive a call from Geoff. We talked for over an hour and he asked if I'd like to get together on Saturday. I accepted, and we spent the afternoon touring the Isabella Gardner Museum in Boston, followed by dinner. Although I had been warned by family and friends not to tell Geoff about my eating disorder or battle with depression, I felt it was only right to let him know about me. I mean, how many times could we go out to eat before he would notice I had "a thing about eating"? Today, looking back at the situation, I also think that because I was afraid of getting into a relationship with anyone, I felt it would be better to scare him off than have to traverse in an area I knew nothing about.

I vividly remember sitting on the sofa in the "living room" section of my studio apartment and telling Geoff about my battle with anorexia nervosa and the episodes of major depression. He listened and after I was through, took my hand, looked directly at me and told me he was sorry that I had to suffer through the times I did, but he was not going anywhere. This positive, supportive response was not supposed to happen! OK—now what?

From our very first meeting in May 1999 to the trip to his mother's home in Orlando that December, Geoff would not let my eating disorder get in the way of *us*. Imagine my terror at the thought of meeting his mother and two brothers, one of whom is a psychologist. Would they think I was too fat, ugly or stupid? Before I left for our trip to Florida a few friends and my mom predicted that I would come back with an engagement ring. I just laughed at them.

Geoff's mom had a small New Year's eve party—after all this was the big one—1999 was giving way to 2000 and everyone was anticipating something BIG! The television was on and we watched the ball fall at Times Square before proceeding to the balcony at his mom's apartment to view the fireworks at Disney. With a glass of wine in each hand (provided by Geoff's brothers) I watched the fireworks thinking, *"I wonder where Geoff went?"*

Suddenly, I felt Geoff at my side with his lips to my ear asking me what "I would think about changing my name come July or August?" Not quite believing what had just happened, he ushered me into the living room and asked me if I would mind taking off the ring I had been wearing on the middle finger of my left hand. Still kind of dazed, I took the ring off and he slipped a gorgeous diamond ring on my finger and kissed me. I could not believe that this was happening to me. When his family came into the living room griping about how nothing big happened as we entered into a new century, I told them they were mistaken and held out my hand. His mom cried out, "I was hoping he was going to ask you to marry him!" Yes, I had passed muster with his family, and they were happy for us. In fact, several years after our marriage, Geoff's mom thanked me for giving her son back to her; she explained that after his first wife's death, Geoff had been so sad, but now he smiled.

I was 45 on my wedding day, August 12, 2000 and at the ages of 71 and 80, my mom and dad walked me down the aisle to my new life.

Sadly, as I began to grow emotionally, my new-found voice collided with Geoff's strong personality and we ended up divorcing, at my choice, after 10 years of marriage.

Inexplicable Weight Gain

Shortly after my engagement to Geoff, I gave up my apartment in Brighton, Massachusetts and joined him in the hills of New Hampshire. Moving from the Boston area, which was alive with arts, culture, and friends, for the comparatively small sleepy city of Milford, New Hampshire, was the price I paid for love. I was unable to secure employment, missed my friends, and spent my days doing very little until I got the bright idea to join Gold's Gym in Nashua, New Hampshire to shape and tone up for my wedding day. The drive to the gym was about half an hour from Milford, so at least I got to see some different scenery. Yes, I worked out and much to my dismay, the scale started going up, not down, and I did not feel or look as if I were toning up. I was unhappy and perplexed at the results of my noble efforts. No, I was not eating any more than I had been in Massachusetts. In fact, I was probably eating less. Because Geoff ate his "big meal" at noon in his employer's cafeteria, I generally ate a healthy choice frozen dinner for my evening meal. I ate cottage cheese for breakfast and skipped lunch on most days, so how was I gaining weight? On August 12, 2000, the day of my wedding, I weighed 130 pounds and felt like a beached whale as I walked down the aisle.

Two days after our wedding, Geoff and I took off for a three-week honeymoon in Hawaii. As always, my eating was precise and I drooled while Geoff indulged in cocktails, appetizers, and desserts. The only dessert I truly tasted was a fruit and ice cream dish called a "Carmen Miranda," one evening at the end of our honeymoon. During our sojourn to Hawaii we ate breakfast in our room (I had cottage cheese and fruit while Geoff had cereal with fruit), skipped lunch most days (on days we had lunch, I ate dry tuna from cans I had packed), and ate fish for dinner at a restaurant with the ocean and setting sun as a backdrop. As soon as we arrived home from our honeymoon I stepped on the scale only to see that it had increased by seven pounds. I was distraught. NO WAY in the world could I have gained this much weight given my meager portions.

Geoff saw my anguish and agreed that I should seek advice from a doctor. I connected with a family practitioner in New Hampshire and after taking my history, examining me, and obtaining blood work, she sent me to both an endocrinologist and hematologist. This was in December 2000. I was anemic (nothing new) and although my thyroid appeared "normal" the doctor could not fathom why I had gained weight.

After testing, the hematologist was at a loss to explain my anemia (not from iron deficiency) and suggested that perhaps all the years of "starving" had caused a "depression" in my bone marrow. She was considering a bone marrow biopsy for the future and it was my decision to put it off for as long as possible. After all, I had been anemic for as long as I could remember.

In addition to all sorts of blood tests, the endocrinologist ordered a CT scan of my pituitary gland to check for a possible tumor. My TSH was normal and my Free T4 was slightly low. She was considering putting me on a low dose of thyroid medication to see if this would help stop the weight gain.

It was at this time that due to work circumstances, my husband upset the apple cart with an unscheduled move to Florida. Upon our move to Florida I reviewed the listing of endocrinologists who were on our insurance plan and called several in hope of finding one who had experience treating people like myself—those who gain weight despite eating a low-calorie diet.

Unfortunately for me, the endocrinologist I selected was a total jerk. Although I was his first appointment after lunch, he strolled in 45 minutes late and barely looked at me. I handed him the office notes from the endocrinologist in New Hampshire. He did not even look at the notes. After briefly listening, he told me I was eating more than I thought I was and simply needed to eat less and exercise more. When I tried to tell him otherwise, he laughed and left the room. HELP ME! I was crying hysterically and told his office staff that he mistreated me. When I got the bill for my co-payment, I refused to pay. I called the office and told them to save their postage as I was not going to pay. After months of trying to collect and threatening me with small claims court, they finally figured it wasn't worth the time or trouble.

Still being frustrated and gaining more weight, I sought help from another endocrinologist. Although this doctor was nicer, he too explained that as we get older we need to eat less and I should just accept it and move on. Yeah, right.

So, the days passed by and the pounds kept piling on and I was miserable. I did an internet search for nutritionists with expertise in eating disorders. I found one in Winter Park, Florida (only 100 miles from our condo) and decided it was worth the trip. Incidentally, my late mother-in-law just so happened to reside in Winter Park at this time, so I would also pay a visit to her. Geoff took off from work to accompany me to my first appointment with Karen Beerbower. She assured us that she had dealt with clients such as myself before and was certain she could help me. Well, I schlepped to Winter Park on a regular basis for over a year and did not lose an ounce. The nutritionist gave me no advice on what to eat—she kept telling me that I had to eat more to lose weight and just throw away the scale and stop worrying. Easier said than done.

Tenaciousness being one of my qualities, I found Barbara Corell, a nutritionist in Clearwater, Florida only 16 or so miles from home. Barbara believed she could help me and I believed in her. I followed every eating plan she developed for me and still did not lose weight.

OK, now I had wasted time, money, and energy and was still struggling with this weight gain. I entered therapy for a short time with Dr. Lia Nardone, the psychiatrist who prescribed and monitored my antidepressant medication and all I could focus on was the weight. Not quite knowing what to do, in January of 2004, Dr. Nardone referred me to Dr. Pauline Powers, an internationally-renowned psychiatrist and authority on eating disorders at the University of South Florida in Tampa.

After interviewing me and analyzing the results of psychological testing she suggested that I increase my antidepressant (at that time it was Prozac) to 60 mg., add a booster of 25 micrograms of Cytomel, and increase my calories ("I think you need to increase your calories even though this seems counterintuitive. I suspect that you have reduced your calories so low that your body is conserving energy rather than expending it"). Although I respected Dr. Powers, I did not want to increase my antidepressant or add another drug to the mix. Also, I could not bring myself to simply eat more.

I continued to suffer and obsess about what I ate and didn't eat. It was difficult to watch other people on diets eat more than I ate and see their diminishing size. What now? I joined Curves for Women and was a faithful member, exercising a minimum of three days a week. Though I lost inches, I failed to lose pounds.

One day, while reading *Readers Digest,* I was intrigued with an article written by Dr. Wayne Callaway, an endocrinologist in Washington, DC. who stated that he had helped people with all types of eating problems. I called his office and asked a myriad of questions and was convinced that he was going to be the answer to all my problems. Geoff was not as gung-ho as me, but feeling my pain, he agreed to indulge me in a whirlwind trip to DC. We left on an early-morning flight to arrive in time for a mid-morning appointment with Dr. Callaway. After a lengthy meeting with the doctor and fancy oxygen consumption, body analysis, and blood tests, Dr. Calloway recommended that I begin taking a drug called Glucophage. He suggested that my insulin level might be a factor in my weight gain. Being a good patient, I took the Glucophage but had adverse effects. I became shaky, weepy and sweaty. I had to discontinue the Glucophage and because the distance between Florida and DC is so great, it was impractical for me to continue treatment with Dr. Callaway.

In October of 2004, my fibroid tumors grew large enough to press on my bladder and surrounding organs. Since I had undergone two prior myomyectomies for removal of fibroids, my only choice at this juncture was to have a complete hysterectomy. I liked and trusted my gynecologist Dr. Debra Hemsath and had previously shared with her my frustration over my weight dilemma. It was during an exam after my hysterectomy that I again spoke to Dr. Hemsath about my weight. She posited the idea that perhaps I needed a low dose of thyroid medication and referred me to Dr. Lee Alice Goscin, an endocrinologist.

Ugh—another doctor to whom I had to explain my story. Dr. Goscin listened to me, examined me and pointedly told me that she believed she could help me, but I would have to be patient. Initially, although she disagreed with my eating only 1000–1200 calories, she tried to help me balance my eating regimen with the correct percentage of carbs, protein and fats. I lost about ¼ pound in 3 months, another ½ pound in another 3 months and so on. Never did this wonderful doctor tell me that I was eating too much or "I had to simply accept the weight and move on." At some point she added a low dose of thyroid medication to my regimen. Albeit slowly, my weight began to gown down. Still not happy with the slow results, I spoke to Dr. Goscin and she ordered a fasting glucose blood test. The results showed that my sugar was fine but that my insulin level was elevated—a condition called hyperinsulinemia. Dr. Callaway was moving in the right direction. In simple terms, hyperinsulinemia is an abnormally high level of insulin in the blood which can result in increased weight gain! Finally, an answer.

I cannot tell you the joy I felt when told there was a reason other than food for my weight gain. Working with Dr. Goscin and taking a low dose of thyroid medication as well as Glucophage for the hyperinsulinemia and doing Pilates regularly resulted in weight loss as well as muscle toning. Though the weight came off painfully slow, the results were evident. That is, evident to an extent…

Although I could fit into small sized clothing, the number on the scale was not the "magic" number I selected for my ideal weight and I continued to strive to reach my goal. Others told me I was not fat, but the picture I saw of myself told me differently.

A Misguided Doctor

In 1996 I had abdominal surgery for the removal of a large fibroid tumor that was pressing on nearby organs. After the surgery, my abdomen was *very* distended and bruised. I was in pain and concerned at how disfigured I appeared. In no way were my thoughts associated with the eating disorder. However, as unfair as it may be, some medical practitioners misinterpret the concerns of a patient when that patient also has a psychiatric illness such as anorexia nervosa as part of their medical history.

I had the unpleasant experience of meeting such an individual in the guise of a resident who was making rounds for my attending physician. This cocky young man came into my room, stood by my bed, and asked me how I was feeling as he poked and surveyed my distended abdomen. I mentioned my shock at the sight of my swollen abdomen and without missing a beat, he said "I'm a surgeon, not a psychiatrist, I can't help you with your body image problems." What ignorance and sheer chutzpah on his part. Shocked at his response, I said nothing. When he left the room, I cried and confided my dissatisfaction about this insensitive doctor with the nurse. She tried to be of comfort and told me that she had seen him in action before and his bedside manner left a lot to be desired. She agreed that he never should have said anything relating to a diagnosis that I was not being treated for during the hospitalization. Truthfully, during the admission process, I did not mention anything about my eating disorder history, but I have a feeling it sticks with you like a fly on wallpaper.

To his credit, before my discharge, the offending doctor stopped by to apologize. Apparently, the nurse told him he was out of line. However, the way I see it, the incident never should have happened.

Eating Disorders Shared By Roommates

As a young woman living on a "shoestring budget" in Boston, Massachusetts in the early 1980s it was necessary to share an apartment with roommates. After sharing an apartment with two other young women who did not care if garbage literally sat in the middle of the kitchen, I decided to seek an alternative living arrangement.

I became a "boarder" in an apartment rented by an elderly woman, Mrs. Plovnick. Though the lease was in her name, she rented two spare rooms to "decent" women. At this point in my life my needs were simple. I was literally doing no cooking and subsisting on shredded cabbage, D-Zerta gelatin, carrots, and a large delicious apple. The apple was a treat eaten in secret each night as I sat in a warm bath. I did not want anyone to see me eating. God only knows why, but now I can look back and imagine it had something to do with looking like I was weak for eating the "forbidden" fruit.

It was during this period of time that my dear friend Toby packed up and moved to New York to begin her new life as a married lady. Not having anyone to hang out with after work and on weekends, I stayed close to home. Mrs. Plovnick was a nice woman and sometimes I conversed with her or just stayed in my room.

Shortly after I moved into the apartment, another "boarder" moved out and a young woman named Hope moved in. Hope was considerably younger than me and I found her entertaining. Fresh out of school she had no idea what she wanted to do and for the time-being was working as a sales person at Saks Fifth Avenue. Though we didn't socialize together, in the apartment she was good company.

On several occasions Hope pleaded with me to eat. She confronted me with the truth, which by now I was aware of—I had anorexia nervosa and she was afraid I was going to die. I assured her I was getting help and there was no need to worry. Eventually, living with me and an elderly woman became too much for Hope to bear and she moved out.

After she left I was sad and asked myself what I was doing in such an environment and came to the conclusion that I, too, needed to make a change in my living accommodations. I searched the newspaper for apartments and was thrilled to find one right across the street. When I went to look at the apartment and interview the person looking for a roommate, I received a warm welcome and decided to move in.

Susan, my roommate, never told me that she was bulimic, but through a series of events I learned that I was not the only one in the apartment struggling with an eating disorder. At this point in my recovery I was eating more than diet gelatin, cabbage, carrots, and an apple. I ate cottage cheese, bran cereal, Laughing Cow cheese, and a mixture of squash, zucchini, and onions I cooked in tomato juice.

When I opened my box of bran cereal I measured it into individual servings which I placed in plastic sandwich bags secured with a twist tie. The bags were then stuffed inside the box and were ready when I decided to eat some. When I made the vegetable dish I would cool it on the counter before placing it in the refrigerator. Already individually wrapped at the factory, the cheese needed no preparation.

I was very exacting with what and when I ate and was puzzled when my food began to disappear. From bags of cereal to a whole package of cheese, my food simply vanished. I confronted Susan with my observation and her answer was that probably when the vegetables cooled they settled which caused them to look like there was less. To her credit, she did tell me that her boyfriend John ate the whole package of cheese and she was sorry. Still, something didn't feel right and it bothered me. Dr. Gordon listened to my dilemma and asked me if I was sure I wasn't eating more than I thought. Incensed, I said NO!

Susan worked out regularly at the gym and was forever brushing her teeth, something I didn't think about until one day after I had a phone conversation with her mother. Susan's mom called when Susan was out and after leaving a message with me, she thanked me. For what? She explained that the family thought Susan had recovered from bulimia until a recent family birthday dinner for her dad proved them wrong. With everyone full, her mom left the cake in the kitchen for "later." When the family decided it was time for birthday cake, they were shocked to find half the cake gone. Yep, Susan had eaten it. Her mom was saddened and offered me her apologies for anything of mine Susan may have eaten.

When I look back at this roommate experience, I can't help but feel that when I came to look at the apartment and Susan saw me (I weighed about 97 pounds and had an orange-yellowish cast to my skin), she was happy that I would not have a lot of food in the house.

After feeling relieved (but sad for Susan) that I was not going crazy or eating my food without realizing it, I decided it was time to move again. As luck would have it, there was a vacant apartment in the building next door (this would make my third address on one street— I bet the mailman loved me!) and I opted to take it and handpick a roommate for myself.

During this time, I was attending a group for people suffering from anorexia nervosa and bulimia. The group was sponsored by Anorexia Bulimia Care of Massachusetts and we met weekly. Another group member, Maureen, who suffered with both anorexia nervosa and bulimia, was living with an elderly woman. The group encouraged her to find a living arrangement with people her own age. Boy, did I have an apartment for her! Although the group tried to dissuade us, Maureen moved in with me. We thought we could help each other.

Appearance wise, Maureen and I were totally opposite. She was tall, very thin and wore lots of make-up and dressed like a European high fashion model. I was short, thin (though I believed I was fat), wore no make-up, and dressed in business clothes appropriate for working in downtown Boston.

Each living in her own eating disordered world which involved competition, denial, support, and frustration, we survived as roommates for about 2 years before Maureen claimed herself recovered and moved out to live in a one-bedroom apartment in the same building. As I'm writing this I just realized that at that point in time, there were three eating disordered people living on Colliston Road in Brighton, Massachusetts (at least three that I knew about).

When Hunger Strikes But the Scale Rules

Often, people will marvel at the anorexic's ability to "not feel hunger." Although it is true that at some point hunger pangs do subside, this is not to say that an anorexic or any other individual is devoid of feeling hunger when food is scarce.

However, unlike most human beings, the individual suffering from anorexia nervosa finds ways to curb their appetite.

Personally, I employed (and sadly, from time to time still do) several strategies. At the height of my illness when I felt that eating anything but my self-prescribed diet was impossible, I would "cut" my hunger with condiments such as paprika, mustard, and sweet 'n low. Eaten by themselves without anything to absorb the odious taste, these substances are tongue curdling.

A "treat" I concocted on my own was to take a bit of cocoa, sweetener and mix in hot water which created my version of hot chocolate. No nutritive value, but something to "sink my teeth into" so to speak.

When the hunger became unbearable, I simply chewed up food and spit it out. I found this act to be helpful, especially if I was stressed.

Never assume that the person with anorexia nervosa is immune from feeling the basic instinct of hunger.

What If Things Had Been Different

One thing any former employer would tell you about me is that I was (and still am) a dedicated employee. Long ago my parents instilled a work ethic into me that still exists. Rather than go to a job, I lived the job giving it 100+ percent of my efforts.

After college, my first real job (other than as a feature writer with the *Huguenot Herald*) was as a Medicare Representative with Blue Cross Blue Shield of Massachusetts (BCBS). It was during my five-year tenure with BCBS that I was officially diagnosed with anorexia nervosa and began outpatient treatment. Over the years, I made several lateral job transfers at BCBS and was consistently passed over for promotions despite my favorable reviews.

While working as a "provider representative" in Professional Contracts, I struck up a friendship with one of the vice president's daughters who would work during the summer or holiday breaks. I had no idea she (or anyone else) knew about my eating disorder.

One day my supervisor told me the vice president wanted to see me in his office. I was perplexed—was I in trouble? When I arrived at his office he was welcoming and told me his daughter consistently asked for me and how I was. He then asked me if I was well. He went on to point out that I was very thin, and he was concerned lest I had cancer or some other dreaded malady. I assured him I did not and confided in him my diagnosis of anorexia nervosa and told him I was in therapy and everything would be fine. He told me he thought I was talented and if I took care of myself I would certainly do well at BCBS.

Therapy continued, I did better, and consequently, a job was created for me. I still spent time in Professional Contracts but was also given the task of writing a bi-weekly newsletter for the professional relations representatives who visited physicians' offices. In addition,

I helped plan and wrote about BCBS's first computer exhibition in 1983.

I applied for several promotions (all involving writing skills) and was passed over each time. After one such rejection, I spoke candidly to the vice president and asked him if he thought I was "blackballed" because of my "illness." He uncomfortably told me he believed the latest job rejection had been a "bag job"—they already had a candidate in mind when the job was posted. He also agreed that due to my diagnosis, I would probably never advance at BCBS.

When I decided to terminate my employment with BCBS he offered me support and recommendations.

After several months working for a temporary agency, the Bank of Boston offered me a permanent job. They "bought out" my contract with the agency and I worked in the bank's Chinatown branch; ultimately ending up in the Coolidge Corner branch in Brookline, Massachusetts.

While at the Coolidge Corner Branch I had two medical leaves of absence for anorexia nervosa. My coworkers and management were aware of my condition for which I was hospitalized.

Again, irrespective of my illness, I was a top performer, going above and beyond my job description of administrative assistant. To be sure, some months I even beat out customer service representatives for bringing in the most dollars for new account openings.

Again, five years and no promotions. When I finally broached the topic with one of the female vice presidents, it once again became apparent that my eating disorder had kept me from professional advancement.

I left the bank and searched around, temped, and searched some more. At this time, I was still in therapy for anorexia nervosa (my weight was "normal low") and depression. I remember one of the job interviewers telling me that I had it all except I didn't smile. Yeah, right, easy for him to say.

Through a roommate, I ended up working as an administrative assistant to Richard M. Rose, MD, Chief of Pulmonary Medicine at the New England Deaconess Hospital (now, Beth Israel Deaconess Medical Center). Rich was a kind man with a big heart.

In addition to handling Rich's academic and clinical calendars, I did literature searches, edited manuscripts and coordinated the Fellowship Training Program.

At some point, Rich sat down with me and told me he was concerned about me. He sensed that I was suffering from depression and urged me to get help. After discussing it with him and my therapist, I did take a two week leave and entered the hospital for treatment. Probably a good move for me personally, but a bust professionally. Rich and his wife Mary Ann were supportive of me but unfortunately, not the rest of the system.

Rich was offered a dream position in La Jolla, California and both he and Mary Ann tried to convince me to move with them. Although I respected them and appreciated their belief in me, I felt that to move to California to be an administrative assistant was not in my best interest.

I stayed on as administrative assistant to the interim chief until funding ran out and then laterally transferred to the Department of Internal Medicine as assistant to the Chief of Medicine. This job was not to my liking and I applied for various writing positions within the hospital only to be rejected.

Once again, it appeared that my eating disorder and its related depression had messed up my chance for professional advancement.

I decided to cut my losses and start anew. With my eyes set on obtaining a Masters in Public Health, I applied for and accepted a position at Boston University School of Medicine. I got a bit of a raise and tuition reimbursement to boot—how much better could it be?

Unfortunately, I worked for a physician who went through assistants like cameras at the time went through film. Although the personnel department was aware of the "revolving door" of workers going through his office, their hands were tied because he was an endowed chair who brought in big money to the university. I tried transferring to another position without luck. After 13 months of hell with this boss, I left the university without a job.

As a result of workplace stress, my condition deteriorated, and I had to be hospitalized for major depression. After the treatment and time to heal, I looked for employment and settled for a position as Camp Coordinator for Camp Joslin run by Boston's Joslin Diabetes Center.

Perhaps I had moved too fast. Although I showed up for work every day and gave it my all—staying late and working weekends when needed—my spirit was low. Call me naïve, stupid, or a little of each—I confided in my boss that I felt as though I was having a relapse of depression and that was the beginning of my end at the job.

Despite the fact that I was told I was doing a great job, when my three-month evaluation came up, I was told that my performance was unsatisfactory and was asked to resign. In all of my years of working I had never been hurt so badly. I cried and tried to defend myself and simply could not do anything. I signed the paper and fell further into the depths of depression. By the way—my stint at Joslin never appeared on my resume and until now, very few people knew about it. Welcome to my secret life.

During this time, I dated and married a man who could best be described as controlling. Although we stayed married for 10 years, as I began recovery from the depression and eating disorder, I became a stronger woman—a woman who didn't like being controlled.

The year 2010 will forever remain etched in my mind as the most horrific of my life as this was when my divorce became final, I lost my job, and my beloved father passed away. Not surprisingly, all of the sorrowful events took their toll on my emotional and physical health and I was once again fighting major depression as well as anorexia nervosa.

After several friends confronted me with the fact that they thought I had a problem, I owned up to it and found the Fairwinds Treatment Center just as they were beginning a newly-established Intensive Outpatient Treatment Program (IOP). On March 14, 2011, I joined the program and was flabbergasted when several weeks later, Dr. Vicki Berkus, then Director of Eating Disorders at Fairwinds, approached me about going inpatient. It had been over 20 years since my last hospitalization for the anorexia and I did not deem myself sick enough to enter a facility.

However, on May 2, 2011, I courageously left my pride at the front door and entered Fairwinds for a four-week course of treatment. It was here that I believe my true "recovery" from the anorexia took place. Participating in every group and following the nutritional guidelines was difficult but I knew this was my last attempt at establishing a "normal" lifestyle for myself. It is at Fairwinds that I learned what "normal" eating is. Though it was difficult consuming three meals and three snacks daily, I gave into the voice that said otherwise and ate and enjoyed foods I had never dreamed of eating. I found out that I like baked sweet potatoes and Rice Krispie Treats, among other foods. On the rare occasion when I could not finish my meal or snack, I willingly drank a supplement to make up for the missed calories. All in all, my initial stay at Fairwinds was a success!

Because anorexia nervosa and other eating disorders are insidious, I wasn't aware when I "fell off the wagon." Feeling embarrassed and like a failure I sought help from Fairwinds again on August 15, 2011. This time, due to insurance constraints, I was a day patient and for 28 days from 7:00 a.m. until 6:00 p.m., spent my time immersed in a myriad of therapies. This time I believed I really had "recovery" under my belt.

All seemed to be humming along rather smoothly (I had even given my scale to my psychiatrist for safe keeping) as I tried to practice the tools given to me while at Fairwinds.

In February, 2012, my antidepressant needed a boost and unfortunately one of the medications I was prescribed left me with thoughts of suicide. I spent one and one-half days in a psychiatric unit of a general hospital and upon release was readmitted to Fairwinds for two weeks followed by a month of IOP.

Since my last stay at Fairwinds, I have begun living life more fully. Although my treatment team is disappointed that I purchased another scale and weigh myself daily, I am able to socialize on a level like never before. Yes, food remains a touchy subject and some days are better than others but all in all I am maintaining a "healthy" weight while exercising moderately.

Life Today

Although I have come light-years in my struggle with anorexia nervosa, I cannot say that I am completely recovered. I still think about and watch every calorie I consume. Consuming only 1200 calories a day does not give me much leeway in my menu selection and certain foods such as pizza, bagels, pasta, and desserts are off-limits. Very seldom will I drink alcoholic beverages, as for me, they are "empty calories."

Am I happy? Yes and no. I am happy that I am no longer starved in the literal sense. However, there are still many occasions when I do not give into my pains of hunger. Rather than eat, I will chew gum. I'm not by any means proud of this, but it is what it is.

I exercise regularly and weigh myself daily. The number on the scale still dictates if my day begins with a smile or a frown of disgust. I still find it difficult to eat in front of people, and depending on the situation, I might forgo a social event to avoid the meal.

Also, being at a "normal" weight is difficult in that those looking at me from the outside have no idea I am plagued by the anorexic mindset. When someone tells me I look good, I hear them saying, you look fat. Recently, I sat crying while deciding if I could have a small dish of vanilla Dairy Queen with my dear brother Barry.

Will I ever be "normal" concerning food? I guess that depends on one's definition of "normal." Although I would like to be less rigid about food and be able to enjoy food without having the calorie counter in my brain tick off numbers, I doubt that I will ever find peace with food and the bathroom scale.

Considering from whence I came, I guess this is OK. Perhaps it's a matter of whether the glass is half empty or half full. At one point in my existence, I had no "life." Today, despite my preoccupation with food, I am able to find some enjoyment in "life." I have friends and the desire to live despite my anorexic tendencies.

What I am trying to say is, recovery is different for each individual. What feels good and acceptable for one person might be unacceptable or unobtainable for another. As long as a person is cognizant of their situation and willing to admit that there is room for improvement, there is always the possibility for increased recovery.

However, it cannot be said or stressed enough --- the sooner an individual suffering from anorexia nervosa is diagnosed and entered into treatment, the greater the chances are for a FULL recovery.

With permission from the National Eating Disorders Association (NEDA), I am including the following information from their website.

When reading this, please keep in mind the importance of obtaining competent medical care as soon as possible.

Warning Signs and Symptoms

The chance for recovery increases the earlier an eating disorder is detected. Therefore, it is important to be aware of some of the warning signs of an eating disorder.

An individual with anorexia generally won't have all of these signs and symptoms at once, and warning signs and symptoms vary across eating disorders, so this isn't intended as a checklist. Rather, it is intended as a general overview of the types of behaviors that may indicate an eating disorder. If you have any concerns about yourself or a loved one, please seek additional medical help.

Emotional and behavioral signs of anorexia nervosa

- Dramatic weight loss

- Dresses in layers to hide weight loss or stay warm

- Is preoccupied with weight, food, calories, fat grams, and dieting

- Refuses to eat certain foods, progressing to restrictions against whole categories of food (e.g., no carbohydrates, etc.)

- Makes frequent comments about feeling "fat" or overweight despite weight loss

- Complains of constipation, abdominal pain, cold intolerance, lethargy, and/or excess energy

- Denies feeling hungry

- Develops food rituals (e.g., eating foods in certain orders, excessive chewing, rearranging food on a plate)

- Cooks meals for others without eating
- Consistently makes excuses to avoid mealtimes or situations involving food
- Expresses a need to "burn off" calories taken in
- Maintains an excessive, rigid exercise regimen – despite weather, fatigue, illness, or injury
- Withdraws from usual friends and activities and becomes more isolated, withdrawn, and secretive
- Seems concerned about eating in public
- Has limited social spontaneity
- Resists or is unable to maintain a body weight appropriate for their age, height, and build
- Has intense fear of weight gain or being "fat," even though underweight
- Has disturbed experience of body weight or shape, undue influence of weight or shape on self-evaluation, or denial of the seriousness of low body weight
- Postpuberty female loses menstrual period
- Feels ineffective
- Has strong need for control
- Shows inflexible thinking
- Has overly restrained initiative and emotional expression

Physical signs of anorexia nervosa

- Stomach cramps, other non-specific gastrointestinal complaints (constipation, acid reflux, etc.)

- Menstrual irregularities—amenorrhea, irregular periods or only having a period while on hormonal contraceptives (this is not considered a "true" period)

- Difficulties concentrating

- Abnormal laboratory findings (anemia, low thyroid and hormone levels, low potassium, low blood cell counts, slow heart rate)

- Dizziness

- Fainting/syncope

- Feeling cold all the time

- Sleep problems

- Cuts and calluses across the top of finger joints (a result of inducing vomiting)

- Dental problems, such as enamel erosion, cavities, and tooth sensitivity

- Dry skin

- Dry and brittle nails

- Swelling around area of salivary glands

- Fine hair on body (lanugo)

- Thinning of hair on head, dry and brittle hair (lanugo)

- Cavities, or discoloration of teeth, from vomiting

- Muscle weakness

- Yellow skin (in context of eating large amounts of carrots)

- Cold, mottled hands and feet or swelling of feet

- Poor wound healing

- Impaired immune functioning

Health Consequences

Eating disorders can affect every organ system in the body. The body is generally resilient at coping with the stress of eating disordered behaviors, and laboratory tests can generally appear perfect even as someone is at high risk of dying. Electrolyte imbalances can kill without warning; so can cardiac arrest. Therefore, it's incredibly important to understand the many ways that eating disorders affect the body.

Cardiovascular system

- Consuming fewer calories than you need means that the body breaks down its own tissue to use for fuel. Muscles are some of the first organs broken down, and the most important muscle in the body is the heart. Pulse and blood pressure begin to drop as the heart has less fuel to pump blood and fewer cells to pump with. The risk for heart failure rises as the heart rate and blood pressure levels sink lower and lower.

  – Some physicians confuse the slow pulse of an athlete (which is due to a strong, healthy heart) with the slow pulse of an eating disorder (which is due to a malnourished heart). If there is concern about an eating disorder, low heart rate should be considered a symptom

- Purging by vomiting or laxatives depletes your body of important chemicals called electrolytes. The electrolyte potassium plays an important role in helping the heart beat and muscles contract, but is often depleted by purging. Other electrolytes, such as sodium and chloride, can also become imbalanced by purging or by drinking excessive amounts of water. Electrolyte imbalances that can lead to irregular heartbeats and possibly heart failure and death.

Gastrointestinal system

- Slowed digestion known as gastroparesis. Food restriction and /or purging by vomiting interferes with normal stomach emptying and the digestion of nutrients, which can lead to:
  - Stomach pain and bloating
  - Nausea and vomiting
  - Blood sugar fluctuations
  - Blocked intestines from solid masses of undigested food
  - Bacterial infections
  - Feeling full after eating only small amounts of food
- Constipation, which can have several causes:
  - Inadequate nutritional intake, which means there's not enough in the intestines for the body to try and eliminate
  - Long-term inadequate nutrition can weaken the muscles of the intestines and leave them without the strength to propel digested food out of the body
  - Laxative abuse can damage nerve endings and leave the body dependent on them to have a bowel movement
- Binge eating can cause the stomach to rupture, creating a life-threatening emergency
- Vomiting can wear down the esophagus and cause it to rupture, creating a life-threatening emergency.
  - Frequent vomiting can also cause sore throats and a hoarse voice.
- When someone makes themselves vomit over a long period of time, their salivary (parotid) glands under the jaw and in front of

the ears can get swollen. This can also happen when a person stops vomiting.

- Both malnutrition and purging can cause pancreatitis, an inflammation of the pancreas. Symptoms include pain, nausea, and vomiting.

Neurological

- Although the brain weighs only three pounds, it consumes up to one-fifth of the body's calories. Dieting, fasting, self-starvation, and erratic eating means the brain isn't getting the energy it needs, which can lead to obsessing about food and difficulties concentrating.

- Extreme hunger or fullness at bedtime can create difficulties falling or staying asleep.

- The body's neurons require an insulating, protective layer of lipids to be able to conduct electricity. Inadequate fat intake can damage this protective layer, causing numbness and tingling in hands, feet, and other extremities.

- Neurons use electrolytes (potassium, sodium, chloride, and calcium) to send electrical and chemical signals in the brain and body. Severe dehydration and electrolyte imbalances can lead to seizures and muscle cramps.

- If the brain and blood vessels can't push enough blood to the brain, it can cause fainting or dizziness, especially upon standing.

Endocrine

- Many hormones needed by the body are made with fat and cholesterol we eat. Without enough fat and calories in the diet, levels of hormones can fall, including:

  - Sex hormones estrogen and testosterone

  - Thyroid hormones

- Lowered sex hormones can cause menstruation to fail to begin, to become irregular or stop completely. This can significantly increase bone loss (known as osteopenia and osteoporosis) and the risk of broken bones and fractures.

- Reduced resting metabolic rate, a result of the body's attempts to conserve energy.

- Over time, binge eating can potentially increase the chances that a person's body will become resistant to insulin, a hormone that lets the body get energy from carbohydrates. This can lead to type 2 diabetes.

- Without enough energy to fuel its metabolic fire, core body temperature will drop and hypothermia may develop.

- Starvation can cause high cholesterol levels, although this is NOT an indication to restrict dietary fats, lipids, and/or cholesterol.

Other

- Low caloric and fat consumption cam cause dry skin, and hair to become brittle and fall out.

- To conserve warmth during periods of starvation, the body will grow fine, downy hair called lanugo.

- Severe, prolonged dehydration can lead to kidney failure.

- Inadequate nutrition can decrease the number of certain types of blood cells.

  – Anemia develops when there are too few red blood cells or too little iron in the diet. Symptoms include fatigue, weakness, and shortness of breath.

  – Malnutrition can also decrease infection-fighting white blood cells.

References:

Brown, CA and Mehler, PS. Medical complications of self-induced vomiting. Eating Disorders. 2013;21(4):287-94.

Brown, CA and Mehler, PS. Successful "Detoxing" From Commonly Utilized Modes of Purging in Bulimia Nervosa. Eating Disorders. 2012; 20(4): 312-20.

Katzman, D. K. (2005). Medical complications in adolescents with anorexia nervosa: a review of the literature. International Journal of Eating Disorders, 37(S1), S52-S59.

Mehler, PS and AE Anderson. Eating Disorders. Baltimore: Johns Hopkins UP, 2010. Print.

Mehler, P. S., & Brown, C. (2015). Anorexia nervosa–medical complications. Journal of eating disorders, 3(1), 1.

Mitchell, J. E., & Crow, S. (2006). Medical complications of anorexia nervosa and bulimia nervosa. Current Opinion in Psychiatry, 19(4), 438-443.

When a patient is diagnosed with an ailment such as diabetes, insurance companies generally cover the medical costs associated with the diagnosis. However, when a diagnosis of anorexia nervosa or other eating disorder is made, insurance companies often place "stumbling blocks" in the way of subscribers seeking coverage.

Although countless individuals, organizations and professionals have lobbied against the inequity of benefits accorded to eating disordered individuals, the road remains long and bumpy for individuals trying to extricate themselves from the clutches of a sometimes fatal ailment.

Insurance

Whether for outpatient therapy, inpatient hospitalization, or anything in between, understanding your insurance policy's benefits and obtaining authorization for the appropriate level of care can be confusing and frustrating.

Note: A parent/guardian can legally act on behalf of a person under 18 without prior approval. If your loved one is over 18, they will need to sign a document letting you work with the insurance company on their behalf, even if you are the parent/guardian and the policy is in your name. A customer care representative at the insurance company should be able to tell you or your loved one what documents need to be submitted to allow another person to act on his/her behalf.

Proper treatment of an eating disorder must address both the psychological and physical aspects of the disorder. Many insurance companies have mental health benefits (also known as behavioral health benefits) under a separate umbrella from their physical health benefits. The passage of mental health parity means that, legally, mental health must be covered on par with physical health. However, the separation can still exist, and behavioral health coverage may even be contracted out to a separate company under the supervision of the insurer. All of this combines to create a confusing patchwork array of coverage and rules that can make obtaining proper care for your loved one difficult.

The first-line of decision making about health plan benefits is typically made by a utilization review manager or case manager. These managers review the requests for benefits submitted by a healthcare provider and determine whether the patient is entitled to benefits under the patient's contract. These decision makers may have no particular expertise in the complex, interrelated medical/mental healthcare needs for an eating disorder. Claims can be rejected outright or approved for only part of the recommended treatment plan. Advance, adequate preparation on the part of the patient or the patient's support people is the best way to maximize benefits. Prepare to be persistent, assertive, and rational in explaining the situation and care needs. Early preparation can avert future coverage problems and situations that leave the patient holding the lion's share of bills.

Common reasons for denying insurance benefits include:

- Weight – typically, that it's not low enough
- Treatment history
  - Patient has not tried a lower level of care prior to requesting a higher level of care
  - Patient's condition is chronic and past treatments at the requested level of care have been ineffective
- Lack of progress in treatment
  - Patient is not restoring weight
  - No reduction in behaviors
  - Lack of motivation in treatment
  - Inconsistent attendance

- Absence of behaviors – treatment is going well, and it may be appropriate to step down in level of care

- No medical complications

Here are some tips to help you obtain the insurance benefits your loved one needs and deserves so that they have the best chance possible to recover from an eating disorder.

Educate yourself

Read through NEDA's resources to learn about eating disorders, treatment, and current clinical practice guidelines, and have them in hand when speaking to your health plan about benefits. Be prepared to ask your health plan for the evidence-based information they use to create their coverage policy for eating disorders.

Read your plan

Obtain a copy of the full plan description from the health plan's member's website, the insurer, or, if the insurance plan is through work, the employer's human resources department. This document may be longer than 100 pages. Do not rely on general pamphlets or policy highlights. Read the detailed description of the benefits contract to find out what is covered and for how long. If you can't understand the information, try talking with the human resources staff at the company that the insurance policy comes through, with an insurance plan representative (the number is on the back of your insurance identification card), or with a billing/claims staff person at facilities where you are considering obtaining treatment. If hospital emergency care is not needed, make an appointment with a physician you trust to get a referral or directly contact eating disorder treatment centers to find out how to get a full assessment and diagnosis. The assessment should consider all related physical and psychological problems. The four main reasons for doing this are:

- To obtain as complete a picture as possible about everything that is wrong

- To develop the best plan for treatment

- To obtain cost estimates before starting treatment

- To obtain the benefits the patient is entitled to under his/her contract for the type of care needed. For example, many insurers provide more coverage benefits for severe mental disorder diagnoses. Some insurers categorize anorexia and bulimia nervosa as severe disorders that qualify for extensive inpatient and outpatient benefits, while others may not.

Medical benefits coverage also often comes into play when treating eating disorder-associated medical conditions, so diagnosing all physical illnesses present is important. Other mental conditions often coexist with an eating disorder and should be considered during the assessment, including depression, trauma, obsessive compulsive disorder, anxiety, social phobias, and chemical dependence. These coexisting conditions can affect eligibility for various benefits (and often can mean more benefits can be accessed) and eligibility for treatment centers.

Document everything

If you don't document it, it didn't happen. It's a saying frequently used in the legal and insurance fields alike. Insurance attorneys recommend documenting every single contact you have with your loved one's insurer, including the time and date of the call, the name of the person with whom you spoke and their contact information, and what was discussed during the conversation. Experts also recommend keeping copies of all written communication you receive from your insurance companies, such as denial or approval letters, explanations of benefits, and more. Some loved ones have found it useful to organize everything in a folder, a binder, or electronically.

If you decide to tape record any conversation, you must first inform and ask the permission of the person with whom you are speaking.

Confirm with the insurer that the patient has benefits for treatment. Also ask about "in-network" and "out-of-network" benefits and the eating disorder facilities that have contracts with the patient's insurance company, because this affects how much of the costs the patient is responsible for. If the insurer has no contract with certain treatment facilities, benefits may still be available, but may be considered out-of-network. In this case, the claims will be paid at a lower rate and the patient will have a larger share of the bill.

You may also want to consider having an attorney in mind at this point in case you need to consult someone if roadblocks appear; however, avoid an adversarial attitude at the beginning. Remember to keep complete written records of all communications with every contact at your insurance company.

Other things to remember:

- Thank and compliment anyone who has assisted you.

- You're more likely to receive friendly service when you are polite while being persistent.

- Send important letters via certified mail to ensure they can be tracked and signed for at the recipient location.

- Set a timeframe and communicate when you would like an answer. Make follow-up phone calls if you have not received a response in that timeframe.

- Don't assume one department knows what the other department is doing. Copy communications to all the departments, including health, mental health, enrollment, and other related departments.

- Don't panic when and if you receive the first denial. Typically, a denial is an automatic computer-generated response that requires a "human override." Often you need to go up at least one level, and perhaps two levels, to reach the decision maker with authority to override the automated denial.

- Your insurance company only knows what you and the treating professionals tell them. Make sure they have all information necessary to make decisions that will be of most benefit to you or your loved one.

- Make no assumptions. Your insurance company is not the enemy – but may be uninformed about your case. Treat each person as though he/she has a tough job to do.

Be aware that if the patient is a college student who had to drop out of school to seek treatment and was covered by school insurance or a parent's insurance policy, the student may no longer be covered if not a full-time student. While many people will continue working or attending school, some cannot. If this is the case, it's important to understand what happens with insurance. Most insurance policies cover students as long as they are enrolled in 12 credit hours per semester and attend classes. Experts in handling insurance issues for patients with eating disorders caution that patients who have dropped out of school should avoid trying to cover up that fact to maintain benefits, because insurance companies will usually find out and then expect the patient to repay any benefits that were paid out.

If coverage has been lost, the student may be eligible to enroll in a Consolidated Omnibus Budget Reconciliation Act (COBRA) insurance program. COBRA is an Act of Congress that allows people who have lost insurance benefits to continue those benefits as long as they pay the full premium and qualify for the program. See www.cobrainsurance.com for more information. A person eligible for COBRA has only 30 days from the time of loss of benefits to enroll in a COBRA plan. It is critical that the sign up for COBRA be done or that option is lost. Be sure to get written confirmation of COBRA enrollment from the plan. If the student is not eligible for

COBRA, an insurance company may offer a "conversion" plan for individual coverage.

Obtain a case manager

A case manager will be a single person at your insurance company who will handle your loved one's case. This can make it easier to contact your insurance company with questions and other issues, since you will only have to make one phone call. As well, this individual will become familiar with your loved one's case, facilitating decision making.

Sample Letters to Insurance Companies

These sample letters from NEDA's website can be used in various circumstances you may encounter that require you to communicate with insurance companies. These letters were developed and used by families who encountered these situations. Keep in mind that a cordial, business communication tone is essential.

Remember:

- Follow up letters with phone calls and document whom you speak to.

- Don't assume one insurance department knows what the other is doing.

- Don't panic! Your current issue or rejection can be a computer generated "glitch."

- Copy letters to others relevant to the request. Also, if you are complimenting someone for the assistance they've provided, tell them you'd love to send a copy to their boss to let him/her know about the great service you've received.

- Supply supporting documents.

- Get a signed delivery receipt – especially when time is of the essence.

- Obtain and insert the name of a person to whom you'll address the letter — avoid sending to a generic title or "To Whom It May Concern."

Sample Letter #1

Request that the copay for the psychiatrist from the patient be changed to a medical copay rate instead of the higher mental health copay, because the psychiatrist was providing medication management, not psychotherapy.

Outcome: Adjustments can be made so that the family is billed for the medical copay. Remember, the psychiatrist must use the proper billing code.

Date:

To: NAME OF CONTACT PERSON

INS. CO. NAME & ADDRESS

From: YOUR NAME & ADDRESS

Re: PATIENT'S NAME

DOB (Date of Birth)

Insurance ID#

Dear [NAME],

Thank you for assisting me with [my/my loved one's] medical care. As you can imagine, this process is very emotionally draining on the entire family. However, the cooperation of the fine staff at [INSURANCE COMPANY NAME] makes it a little easier.

At this time, I would like to request that [INS. CO.] review the category that [Dr. NAME's] services have been placed into. It appears that I am being charged a copay for [his/her] treatment as a mental health service when in reality [he/she] provides [PATIENT NAME] with pharmacologic management for [his/her] neuro-bio-chemical disorder. Obviously, this is purely a medical consultation. Please review this issue and kindly make adjustments to past and future consultations.

Thank you in advance for your cooperation and assistance.

Sincerely,

[YOUR NAME] Cc: [list the people in the company you are sending copies to]

Sample Letter #2

The need to flex hospital days for counseling sessions. Remember, just because you are using outpatient services does not mean that you cannot take advantage of benefits for a more acute level of care if your child is eligible for that level of care. The insurance company only knows the information you supply, so be specific and provide support from the treatment team!

Outcome: 10 Hospital days were converted to 40 counseling sessions.

Date:

To: NAME OF CONTACT PERSON

INS. CO. NAME & ADDRESS

From: YOUR NAME & ADDRESS

Re: PATIENT'S NAME

DOB (Date of Birth)

Insurance ID#

Case #

Dear [NAME]:

This letter is in response to [insurance company name's] denial of continued counseling sessions for my [daughter/son]. I would like this decision to be reconsidered because [insert PATIENT NAME] continues to meet the American Psychiatric Association's clinical practice guidelines criteria for Residential treatment/Partial hospitalization. [His/Her] primary care provider, [NAME], supports [his/her] need for this level of care (see attached – Sample Letter #3 provides an example of a physician letter). Therefore, although [he/she] chooses to receive services from an outpatient team, [he/she] requires an intensive level of support from that team, including ongoing counseling, to minimally meet [his/her] needs. I request that you correct the records re: [PATIENT NAME's] level of care to reflect [his/her] needs and support these needs with continued counseling services, since partial hospitalization / residential treatment is a benefit [he/she] is eligible for and requires.

I am enclosing a copy of the APA guidelines and have noted [PATIENT NAME'S] current status. If you have further questions you may contact me at: [PHONE#] or [Dr. NAME] at: [PHONE#].

Thank you in advance for your cooperation and prompt attention to this matter.

Sincerely,

[YOUR NAME]

Cc: [Case manager]

[Ins. Co. Medical manager]

Sample Letter #3

Letter to a managed care plan to seek reimbursement for services that the patient received when time was insufficient to obtain pre-authorization because of the serious nature of the illness and the need to deal with it urgently.

Remember: you need to research the professionals available through your plan and local support systems. In this case, after contacting their local association for eating disorders experts, the family that created this letter realized that no qualified medical experts were in their area to diagnose and make recommendations for their child. Keep in mind that you need to seek a qualified expert, and not a world-famous expert. Make sure you provide very specific information from your research.

Outcome: Reimbursement was provided for the evaluating/treating psychiatrist visits and medications. Further research and documentation was required to seek reimbursement for the treatment facility portion.

DATE

To: NAME OF CONTACT PERSON

INS. CO. NAME & ADDRESS

From: YOUR NAME & ADDRESS

Re: PATIENT'S NAME

DOB (Date of Birth)

Insurance ID#

Case #

Dear [NAME]:

My [son/daughter] has been under treatment for [name the eating disorder and any applicable co-existing condition] since [month/year]. [He/she] was first seen at the college health clinic at [UNIVERSITY NAME] and then referred for counseling that was arranged through [INS. CO.]. At the end of the semester I met with my [son/ daughter] and [his/her] therapist to make plans for treatment over the summer. At that time, residential treatment was advised, which became a serious concern for us. We then sought the opinion of a qualified expert about this advice. I first spoke to [PATIENT NAME'S] primary physician and then contacted the local eating disorders support group. No qualified expert emerged quickly from the community of our [INS. CO.] network providers. In my research to identify someone experienced in eating disorder evaluation and treatment, I discovered that [insert Dr.NAME at HOSPITAL in LOCATION] was the appropriate person to contact to expedite plans for our child. Dr. [NAME] was willing to see [him/her] immediately, so we made those arrangements.

As you can imagine, this was all very stressful for the entire family. Since continuity of care was imperative, we went ahead with the process and lost sight of the preapproval needed from [INS. CO.]. I am enclosing the bills we paid for those initial visits for reimbursement. [PATIENT NAME] was consequently placed in a residential setting in the [LOCATION] area and continues to see Dr. [NAME] through arrangements made by [INS. CO.].

Also, at the beginning of [his/her] placement, some confusion existed about medications necessary for [PATIENT NAME] during this difficult/acute care period. At one point payment for one of [his/her] medications was denied even though the treatment team recommended it, and it was prescribed by [his/her] primary care physician, Dr. [NAME]. I spoke to a [INS. CO.] employee [insert name] at [PHONE #] to rectify the situation; however, I felt it was a little too late to meet my timeframe for visiting [PATIENT NAME], so I paid for the Rx myself and want reimbursement at this time. If you have any questions, please speak to [employee name].

Thank you in advance for your cooperation. I'd be happy to answer any further questions and can be reached at: [PHONE]

Sincerely,

[YOUR NAME]

Sample Letter #4

To continue insurance while attending college less than full-time so that the student can remain at home for a semester due the eating disorder. Note: When a student does not register on time at the primary university at which he/she has been enrolled, insurance is automatically terminated at that time. Automatic termination can cause an enormous amount of paperwork if not rectified IMMMEDIATELY.

The first letter informs the insurance company of the student's current enrollment status in a timely fashion, and the second letter responds to the abrupt and retroactive termination. Students affected by an eating disorder may be eligible for a medical leave of absence from college for up to one year — so you may want to inquire about that at the student's college.

Outcome: The student was immediately reinstated as a less than full-time student.

DATE

To: NAME OF CONTACT PERSON

INS. CO. NAME & ADDRESS

From: YOUR NAME & ADDRESS

Re: PATIENT'S NAME

DOB (Date of Birth)

Insurance ID#

Case #

Dear [NAME]:

We spoke the other day regarding my [son's/daughter's] enrollment status. I am currently following up on your instructions and appreciate your assistance in explaining what to do. [Dr. NAME] is sending you a letter that should arrive very soon about [PATIENT NAME's] medical status that required [him/her] to reduce the number of classes [he/she] will be able to take this fall. When [he/she] completes re-enrollment at [UNIVERSITY NAME] (which is not possible to do until the first day of classes, [DATE]), [he/she] will have the registrar's office notify you of her status.

At this time, [NAME] plans to be a part-time student at [UNIVERSITY] for the [DATE] semester and plans to return to [UNIVERSITY] in [DATE], provided [his/her] disorder stabilizes. If all goes well, [he/she] may be able to graduate with [his/her] class and complete [his/ her] coursework by the [DATE] in spite of the medical issues. Please feel free to get answers to any questions regarding these plans from [PATIENT NAME'S academic advisor Mr./Ms. NAME], whom [PATIENT NAME] has given written permission in a signed release to speak to you. This advisor has been assisting my [son/daughter] with [his/her] academic plans and is aware of [his/her] current medical status. The advisor's phone number and email are: [PHONE #/ email].

Please feel free to contact me at [PHONE #] if you have any questions or need any further information. Thank you for your assistance.

Sincerely,

[YOUR NAME]

Cc:

Sample Letter #5

Follow-up letter to enrollment department after coverage was terminated retroactive to June 1st by the insurance company's computer.

DATE

To: NAME OF CONTACT PERSON

INS. CO. NAME & ADDRESS

From: YOUR NAME & ADDRESS

Re: PATIENT'S NAME

DOB (Date of Birth)

Insurance ID#

Case #

Dear [NAME]:

I am sure you can imagine my shock at receiving the attached letter [copy of the letter you received] that my [son/daughter] received about termination of coverage. [NAME] has been receiving coverage from [INSURANCE COMPANY] for treatment of serious medical issues since [DATE]. We have received wonderful assistance from [NAME], Case Manager [PHONE#]; [NAME], Mental Health Clinical Director [PHONE#]; and Dr. [NAME], [INS. CO.] Medical Director [PHONE #]. I am writing to describe the timeline of events with copies to the people who have assisted us as noted above.

In [DATE], [PATIENT NAME] requested a temporary leave of absence from [UNIVERSITY 1 NAME] to study at [UNIVERSITY 2 NAME] for one year. [He/she] was accepted at [UNIVERSITY 2 NAME] and attended the [DATE] semester. At the end of the spring semester [PATIENT NAME'S] medical issues intensified and [PATIENT NAME] returned home for the summer. The summer of [YEAR] has been very complicated and a drain on our entire family.

The supportive people noted earlier in this letter made our plight bearable but we were constantly dealing with one medical issue after another.

At the beginning of August [PATIENT NAME] and the treatment team members began to discuss [PATIENT NAME's] needs for the fall semester of [YEAR]. As far as our family was concerned, all options [UNIV. 1, UNIV. 2, & several local options full and part-time] needed to be up for discussion to meet [patient name's] medical needs. We hoped that with the help of [his/her] medical team we could make appropriate plans in a timely fashion.

During [PATIENT NAME's] appointments the first two weeks of August, the treatment team agreed that [PATIENT NAME] should continue to live at home and attend a local university on a part-time basis for the fall semester. This decision was VERY difficult for [PATIENT NAME] and our family. [PATIENT NAME]still hopes/plans to return to [UNIV. 1] in [date] as a full-time student. [He/she] has worked with [his/her] [UNIV. 1] advisor since [date] to work out a plan that might still allow [him/her] to graduate with [his/her] class even if [he/she] needed to complete a class or two in the summer of [YEAR]. This decision by [NAME] was difficult but also a major breakthrough/ necessity for [his/her] treatment.

After a workable plan was made, I called the enrollment department at [INS. CO. NAME] to gain information about the process of notification regarding this change in academic status due to [his/her] current medical needs. [INS. EMPLOYEE NAME] communicated to me that I needed to have my child's primary care physician write a letter supporting these plans. This letter is forthcoming as we speak. As soon as [PATIENT NAME's] fall classes are finalized on [date]' that information will also be sent to you.

In summary, [PATIENT NAME] intended to be a full-time student this fall until [his/her] treatment team suggested otherwise in the early August. At that time I began notifying the insurance company.

Please assist us in expediting this process. I ask that you immediately reinstate [him/her] as a policy member. If [his/her] status is not resolved immediately it will generate a GREAT DEAL of unnecessary extra work for all parties involved and, quite frankly, I'm not sure that our family can tolerate the useless labor when our energy is so depleted and needed for the medical/life issues at hand.

I am attaching 1) my previous enrollment notification note; 2) [PATIENT NAME's] acceptance from [UNIV. 2]; 3) a copy of [PATIENT NAME'S] apartment lease for the year; and 4) [his/her] recent letter to [UNIV. 2] notifying them that [he/she] will be unable to complete the year as a visiting student for medical reasons. Please call me TODAY at [PHONE #] to update me on this issue. This is very draining on our family. Thank you for your assistance.

Sincerely,

[YOUR NAME]

Cc: [CASE MANAGER, MENTAL HEALTH CLINICAL DIRECTOR, MEDICAL DIRECTOR]

Sample Letter #6

Letter from doctor describing any medical complications your child has had, the doctor's recommendations for treatment, and the doctor's prediction of outcome if this treatment is not received. This is a sample physician letter that parents can bring to their child's doctor as a template to work from.

DATE

To: [NAME OF INSURANCE COMPANY MEDICAL DIRECTOR]:

INS. CO. NAME & ADDRESS

From: YOUR NAME & ADDRESS

Re: PATIENT'S NAME

DOB (Date of Birth)

Insurance ID#

Case #

Dear [NAME],

We are writing this letter to summarize our treatment recommendations for [patient name]. We have been following [patient name] in our program since [DATE]. During these past [NUMBER years], [patient name] has had [NUMBER] hospitalizations for medical complications of [insert conditions, e.g., malnutrition, profound bradycardia, hypothermia, orthostasis]. Each of the patient's hospital admissions are listed below [list each and every one separately]:

• Admission Date – Discharge Date [condition]

In all, [patient] has spent [NUMBER] days of the past [NUMBER years] in the hospital due to complications of [his/her] malnutrition. [Patient name's] malnutrition is damaging more than [his/her] heart.

[His/Her] course has been complicated by the following medical issues:

- List each issue and its medical consequence [e.g., secondary amenorrhea since DATE, which has the potential to cause irreversible bone damage leading to osteoporosis in his/her early adult life.]

Despite receiving intensive outpatient medical, nutritional and psychiatric treatment, [patient name's] medical condition has continued to deteriorate with [describe symptoms/signs, e.g., consistent weight loss since DATE] and is currently 83% of [his/her] estimated minimal ideal body weight (the weight where the nutritionist estimates [he/she] will regain regular menses). White blood cell count and serum protein and albumin levels have been steadily decreasing as well, because of extraordinarily poor nutritional intake.

Given this history, prior levels of outpatient care that have failed, and [his/her] current grave medical condition, we recommend that [patient name] urgently receive more intensive psychiatric and nutritional treatment that can be delivered only in a residential treatment program specializing in eating disorders. We recommend a minimum 60- to 90- day stay in a tiered program that offers: intensive residential and transitional components focusing on adolescents and young adults with eating disorders (not older patients). [Patient] requires intensive daily psychiatric, psychologic, and nutritional treatment by therapists well-trained in the treatment of this disease. Such a tiered program could provide the intensive residential treatment that [he/she] so desperately needs so [he/she] can show that [he/she] can maintain any progress in a transitional setting. We do not recommend treatment in a non-eating disorder-specific behavioral treatment center. [Patient]'s severe anorexia requires subspecialty-level care. Examples of such programs would include [name facilities].

Anorexia nervosa is a deadly disease with a 10% to 15% mortality rate; 15% to 25% of patients develop a severe lifelong course. We believe that without intensive treatment in a residential program, [patient name's and condition], and the medical complications that it causes, will continue to worsen causing [him/her] to be at significant risk of developing lifelong anorexia nervosa or dying of the disease. We understand that in the past, your case reviewers have denied [patient] this level of care. This is the only appropriate and medically responsible care plan that we can recommend. We truly believe that to offer a lesser level of care is medically negligent. We trust that you will share our grave concern for [patient's] medical needs and approve the recommended level of care to assist in [his/her] recovery.

Thank you for your thorough consideration of this matter. Please feel free to contact us with any concerns regarding [patient's] care.

Sincerely,

[PHYSICIAN NAME]

Cc: [YOU]

Sample Letter #7

"Discussion" with the insurance company about residential placement when the insurance company suggests that the patient needs to fail at lower levels of care before being eligible for residential treatment. In a telephone conversation, the parents asked the insurance company to place a note in the patient file indicating the insurance company was willing to disregard the American Psychiatric Association guidelines and recommendations of the patient's treatment team and take responsibility for the patient's life. (SEND BY CERTIFIED MAIL!)

Outcome: Shortly thereafter, the parents received a letter authorizing the residential placement.

DATE

To: [NAME OF CEO]

INS. CO. NAME & ADDRESS (use the headquarters)

From: YOUR NAME & ADDRESS

Re: PATIENT'S NAME

DOB (Date of Birth)

Insurance ID#

Case #

Dear [NAME OF INSURANCE COMPANY CEO]:

Residential placement services for eating disorder treatment have been denied for our [son/daughter] against the recommendations of a qualified team of experts consistent with the American Psychiatric Association's evidence-based clinical practice guidelines. Full documentation of our child's grave medical condition and history and our attempts to obtain coverage for that care is available from our case manager [name]. At this time, I would like you to put in writing to me and to my child's case file that [INS. CO.] is taking complete responsibility for my [son's/daughter's] life.

Wendy R. Levine

Respectfully,

[YOUR NAME]

Cc: [CASE MANAGER, NATIONAL MEDICAL DIRECTOR (get the names for both the medical and behavioral health divisions), NATIONAL MEDICAL DIRECTOR – Behavioral Health]

Appeals Process

Continue treatment during the appeals process.

Appeals can take weeks or months to complete, and health professionals and facilities that treat eating disorders advise that it's very important for the patient's well-being to stay in treatment if at all possible to maintain progress in recovery.

Clarify with the insurer the reasons for the denial of coverage.

Most insurers send the denial in writing. Claims advocates at treatment centers advise patients and families to make sure they understand the reasons for the denial and ask the insurance company for the reason in writing if a written response has not been received.

Send copies of the letter of denial to all concerned parties with documentation of the patient's need.

Claims advocates at treatment centers state that sending documentation of an appeals request to the medical director, the human resources director of the company where the patient works (or has insurance under), if applicable, can help bring attention to the situation. Presenting a professional-looking and organized appeal with appropriate documentation, including an evidence-based care plan, makes the strongest case possible. Initial denials are often overturned at higher appeal levels, because higher-level appeals are often reviewed by a doctor who may have a better understanding than the initial claims reviewer of the clinical information provided, especially well-organized, evidence-based documentation.

Ask the insurer what evidence-based outcome measures it uses to assess patient health and eligibility for benefits.

Some insurance companies may use body mass index (BMI) as a criterion for inpatient admission or discharge from treatment for bulimia nervosa, for example, which may not be a valid outcome measure. This is because patients with bulimia nervosa can have close-to-ideal BMIs, when in fact, they may be very sick. Thus, BMI does not correlate well with good health in a patient with bulimia nervosa. For example, if a patient with bulimia nervosa was previously overweight or obese and lost significant weight in a short timeframe, the patient's weight might approach the norm for BMI. Yet, a sudden and large weight loss in such a person could adversely affect his or her blood chemistry and indicate a need for intensive treatment or even hospitalization.

Ask that medical benefits, rather than mental health benefits, be used to cover hospitalization costs for bulimia nervosa-related medical problems.

Claims advocates advise that sometimes claims for physical problems such as those arising from excessive fasting or purging, for example, are filed under the wrong arm of the insurance benefit plan—they are filed under mental health instead of medical benefits. They say it's worth checking with the insurance company to ensure this hasn't happened. That way, mental health benefits can be reserved for the patient's nonmedical treatment needs like psychotherapy. Various diagnostic laboratory tests can identify the medical conditions that need to be treated in a patient with eating disorders. Also, if a patient has a diagnosis of two mental disorders (also called a dual diagnosis), and if that diagnosis is considered by the insurance company to be more "severe" than an eating disorder, the patient may be eligible for more days of treatment.

Cobra Rights Check List

This is a list of requirements that employers must follow to inform their group health plan beneficiaries (employees, spouses, dependents) of their rights under the Consolidated Omnibus Budget Reconciliation Act (COBRA).

Required notices

- Model general and election notices available at www.dol.gov

- General Rights Notice (must be sent within 90 days of enrollment into a group health plan - health, dental, vision, flexible spending account)

- Specific Rights Notice (Election notice - the plan administrator must provide the notice within 14 days after receiving notice of a qualifying event)

- Conversion Rights Notice (must be sent 180 days prior to the end of the maximum continuation period)

- Notice of Unavailability (must be sent when the plan administrator denies coverage after receiving notice and explain why continuation coverage is not available)

- Notice of Termination of COBRA Rights (must be sent when COBRA coverage terminates before the end of the maximum COBRA period)

Enrollment into group health plan

- Send General COBRA notice addressed to covered employee and spouse, if applicable, to home address within 90 days of enrollment into group health plan

- Send General COBRA notice to covered spouse if added during open enrollment or qualified event

Types of qualifying events for COBRA eligibility

- Employee Termination

- Employee Reduction in Hours

- Employee Death

- Entitlement to Medicare

- Employee Divorce or Legal Separation

- Loss of Dependent Child Status

- Length of coverage available

- 18 months (Employee Events)

- 36 months (Dependent Events)

- 29 months (Disability Extension periods)

Payment of COBRA premiums

Premiums are due the first of the coverage month. An administrative charge may be added to the monthly premium. There is a 30-day grace period to make payments. This begins on the second day of the coverage month. For example, September's grace period expires on October 1, not September 30.

Reasons for terminating COBRA coverage

- The maximum continuation period has been reached.

- The Qualified Beneficiary fails to make a timely COBRA premium payment.

- The Qualified Beneficiary is covered under another group health plan AFTER the election of COBRA.

- The Qualified Beneficiary is no longer disabled after the starT of the 11-month extension has begun.

- The Employer ceases to provide any group health coverage to any covered employee.

- The Qualified Beneficiary has become entitled to Medicare, part A or B (For purposes of Medicare, ELIGIBLE means the person has attained the age of 65. ENTITLEMENT means the person has actually become enrolled under Medicare).

Open enrollment

During open enrollment, the same information and enrollment options must be communicated to COBRA Qualified Beneficiaries as to active employees. This includes allowing Qualified Beneficiaries the ability to enroll under a new plan.

The information above was taken from NEDA's website.

For more information on NEDA, visit nationaleatingdisorders.org.

Toll-free Information and Referral Helpline: 1-800-931-2237

The Information and Referral Helpline hours are 9:00 AM - 9:00 PM (ET) Mon-Thurs; and 9:00 AM to 5:00 PM (ET) Fri.

Email: info@NationalEatingDisorders.org

Administrative Office: (212) 575-6200

If the office is closed at the time of your call, please leave a message and someone will return your call as soon as possible.

Fax: (212) 575-1650

Statistics

NEDA has gathered data on the prevalence of eating disorders from the US, UK, and Europe to get a better idea of exactly how common anorexia is. Older data from other countries that use more strict definitions of anorexia and bulimia give lower prevalence estimates:

- In a study of 31,406 Swedish twins born from 1935-1958, 1.2% of the women had strictly defined anorexia nervosa during their lifetime, which increased to 2.4% when a looser definition of anorexia was used (Bulik et al., 2006).

- For twins born between 1975 and 1979 in Finland, 2.2-4.2% of women (Keski-Rahkonen et al., 2007) and 0.24% of men (Raevuori et al., 2009) had experienced anorexia during their lifetime.

- At any given point in time between 0.3-0.4% of young women and 0.1% of young men will suffer from anorexia nervosa

Several more recent studies in the US have used broader definitions of eating disorders that more accurately reflect the range of disorders that occur, resulting in a higher prevalence of eating disorders.

- A 2007 study asked 9,282 English-speaking Americans about a variety of mental health conditions, including eating disorders. The results, published in Biological Psychiatry, found that 0.9% of women and 0.3% of men had anorexia during their life

When researchers followed a group of 496 adolescent girls for 8 years (Stice et al., 2010), until they were 20, they found:

- 5.2% of the girls met criteria for DSM5 anorexia, bulimia, or binge eating disorder.

- When the researchers included nonspecific eating disorder symptoms, a total of 13.2% of the girls had suffered from a DSM-5 eating disorder by age 20.

Combining information from several sources, Eric Stice and Cara Bohon (2012) found that

- Between 0.9% and 2.0% of females and 0.1% to 0.3% of males will develop anorexia

- Subthreshold anorexia occurs in 1.1% to 3.0% of adolescent females

Other statistics related to anorexia:

- Anorexia is the third most common chronic disease among young people, after asthma and type 1 diabetes.

- Young people between the ages of 15 and 24 with anorexia have 10 times the risk of dying compared to their same-aged peers.

- Males represent 25% of individuals with anorexia nervosa, and they are at a higher risk of dying, in part due to the fact that they are often diagnosed later since many people assume males don't have eating disorders.

- Subclinical eating disordered behaviors (including binge eating, purging, laxative abuse, and fasting for weight loss) are nearly as common among males as they are among females.

- An ongoing study in Minnesota has found incidence of anorexia increasing over the last 50 years only in females aged 15 to 24. Incidence remained stable in other age groups and in males.

- Eating disorder symptoms are beginning earlier in both males and females, which agrees with both formal research and clinical reports.

References:

Bennett, D., Sharpe, M., Freeman, C., & Carson, A. (2004). Anorexia nervosa among female secondary school students in Ghana. The British Journal of Psychiatry, 185(4), 312-317.Bulik CM, Sullivan PF, Tozzi F, Furberg H, Lichtenstein P, and Pedersen NL. (2006). Prevalence, heritability, and prospective risk factors for anorexia nervosa. Archives of General Psychiatry, 63(3):305-12. doi:10.1001/archpsyc.63.3.305.

Favaro A, Caregaro L, Tenconi E, Bosello R, and Santonastaso P. (2009). Time trends in age at onset of anorexia nervosa and bulimia nervosa. Journal of Clinical Psychiatry, 70(12):1715-21. doi: 10.4088/JCP.09m05176blu.

Hoek, H. W., & van Hoeken, D. (2003). Review of the prevalence and incidence of eating disorders. International Journal of Eating Disorders, 34(4), 383-396

Hudson, J., Hiripi, E., Pope, H., & Kessler, R. (2007) "The prevalence and correlates of eating disorders in the national comorbidity survey replication." Biological Psychiatry, 61, 348–358.

Keski-Rahkonen A, Hoek HW, Susser ES, Linna MS, Sihvola E, Raevuori A, ..., and Rissanen A. (2007). Epidemiology and course of anorexia nervosa in the community. American Journal of Psychiatry, 164(8):1259-65. doi: 10.1176/appi. ajp.2007.06081388.

Lai, K. Y. (2000). Anorexia nervosa in Chinese adolescents—does culture make a difference?. Journal of Adolescence, 23(5), 561-568.

Lucas AR, Crowson CS, O'Fallon WM, Melton LJ 3rd. (1999). The ups and downs of anorexia nervosa. International Journal of Eating Disorders, 26(4):397-405. DOI: 10.1002/(SICI)1098108X(199912) 26:4<397::AID-EAT5>3.0.CO;2-0.

Mond, J.M., Mitchison, D., & Hay, P. (2014) "Prevalence and implications of eating disordered behavior in men" in Cohn, L., Lemberg, R. (2014) Current Findings on Males with Eating Disorders. Philadelphia, PA: Routledge.

Sabel, A., Rosen, E., & Mehler, P. (2014) "Severe anorexia nervosa in males: clinical presentations and medical treatment." Eating Disorders: The Journal of Treatment and Prevention, 22-3, 209-220.

Stice, E. (2002). Risk and maintenance factors for eating pathology: A meta-analytic review. Psychological Bulletin, 128, 825-848.

Stice E & Bohon C. (2012). Eating Disorders. In Child and Adolescent Psychopathology, 2nd Edition, Theodore Beauchaine & Stephen Linshaw, eds. New York: Wiley.

Stice E, Marti CN, Shaw H, and Jaconis M. (2010). An 8-year longitudinal study of the natural history of threshold, subthreshold, and partial eating disorders from a community sample of adolescents. Journal of Abnormal Psychology, 118(3):587-97. doi: 10.1037/a0016481.

Wade, T. D., Keski-Rahkonen A., & Hudson J. (2011).Epidemiology of eating disorders. In M. Tsuang and M. Tohen (Eds.), Textbook in Psychiatric Epidemiology (3rd ed.) (pp. 343-360). New York: Wiley.

Resources for Individuals and Families

NEDA- National Eating Disorders Association

165 West 46th St.

New York, NY 10036

Phone: (212) 575-6200

Helpline: 1-800-931-237

www.nationaleatingdisordersassociation.org

Supports families whose loved ones are battling eating disorders. Offers the latest information, resources, action-oriented advocacy and media campaigns to educate the public and policymakers and most importantly, a sense of community to people often feeling alone and overwhelmed in their struggle to access quality, affordable care.

ANAD – National Association of Anorexia and Associated Disorders

800 E. Diehl Rd #160

Naperville, IL 60563

Phone: (630) 577-1333

Helpline: (630) 577-1330

www.anad.org

Since 1976 devoted to prevention and alleviation of eating disorders. Provides information about eating disorders.

NEDSP – National Eating Disorder Screening Program

Screening for Mental Health, Inc.

One Washington St., Suite 304

Wellesley Hills, MA 02481

Phone: (781) 239-0071

Email:smjinfo@mentalhealthscreening.org

Mentalhealthscreeningdisorders.org

Offers eating disorder screening programs for colleges and universities, community-based organizations and businesses.

Maudsley Parents

Maudsleyparents.org

Email:contact@maudsleyparents.org

Created in 2006 by parents who helped their children recover with family-based treatment, to offer hope and to help to other families confronting eating disorders. They offer information on eating disorders and family-based treatment, family stories of recovery, supportive parent-to-parent advice and treatment information for families who opt for family based Maudsley treatment.

EDIN – Eating Disorders Information Network

1995 North Park Place

Suite 310N

Marietta, GA 30339

Phone: (404) 465-3385

Myedin.org

A non-profit organization which strives to serve as a comprehensive resource and educational guide for those wanting to learn more about eating disorders and for those seeking help by gathering and distributing information about available treatment options both in Atlanta and nationwide.

MEDA – Multi-Service Eating Disorders Assoc., Inc.

288 Walnut Street

Suite 130

Newtonville, MA 02460

Phone: (617) 558-1881

866-558-6332

Medainc.org

Email: info@medainc.org

Non-profit organization which serves as a resource for those struggling with eating disorders. Dedicated to the prevention and treatment of eating disorders and disordered eating. Serves as a support network and resource for clients, loved ones, clinicians, educators and the general public.

F.E.A.S.T. – Families Empowered and Supporting Treatment of Eating Disorders

P.O. Box 1281

Warrenton, VA 20188

Phone: (855) 503-3278

Feast-ed.org

F.E.A.S.T. is an international organization of and for parents and care givers to help loved ones recover from eating disorders by providing information and mutual support, promoting evidence-based treatment, and advocating for research and education to reduce the suffering associated with eating disorders.

Eating Disorder Hope

P.O. Box 35183

Fort Worth, TX 76162

Phone: (817) 231-5184

www.eatingdisorderhope.com

Founded in 2005 their mission is to offer hope, information and resources to individual eating disorder sufferers their families and treatment providers. Resources include articles on eating disorders, treatment options, support groups, recovery tools and more.

The Elisa Project

10300 N. Central Expy

Suite 330

Dallas, TX 75231

Phone: (866) 837-1999 or (214) 369-5222

theelisaproject.org

Email: tep@theelisaproject.org

Founded in 1999 by Rick and Leslie McCall in memory of their daughter Elisa who suffered from an eating disorder and ultimately took her own life. The Elisa Project is dedicated to the prevention and effective treatment of eating disorders through support, awareness, education and advocacy.

BEDA – Binge Eating Disorder Assoc,

637 Emerson Place

Severna Park, MD 21146

Phone: (855) 855-2332 FAX: (410) 741-3037

Bedaonline.com

Email: info@bedaonline.com

BEDA provides individuals who suffer from binge eating disorder with the recognition and resources they deserve to begin a safe journey toward a healthy recovery. BEDA also serves as a resource for treatment providers to prevent, detect, diagnose, and treat the disorder.

The Alliance for Eating Disorder Awareness

1649 Forum Place #2

West Palm Beach, FL 3340

Phone: 866-662-1235 (561) 841-0900

Email: infor@eatingdisordersinfo.org

Created in 2000 as a source of community outreach, education awareness and prevention of the various eating disorders currently affecting our nation. Through presentations, seminars, workshops, phone and email support, treatment referrals, support groups and information packets, The Alliance offers opportunities for individuals to receive the information they need free of charge.

Remember, **Watch What You Say --- Under any circumstances NEVER EVER TELL an Anorexic that they look good**. As innocent and well intentioned as this statement may be, they will hear it as they are looking FAT!!!! Rather than focus on general appearance, tell them that you like the shirt they are wearing or the way they have done their hair.

Books to Read Concerning Eating Disorders

1. SHADES OF HOPE: HOW TO TREAT YOUR ADDICTION TO FOOD. Tennie McCarty, Berkley Books-Penguin Group, 2012

2. FOOD: THE GOOD GIRL'S DRUG: HOW TO STOP USING FOOD TO CONTROL YOUR FEELINGS. Sunny Sea Gold, Penguin Publishing Group, 2011

3. LIFE BEYOND YOUR EATING DISORDER: Reclaim Yourself, Regain Your Health and Recover For Good. Johana S. Kandel, Harlequin, 2010

4. THE PARENTS' GUIDE TO EATING DISORDERS. Marcia Herrin and Nancy

   Matsumoto, Gurze Books, Second Edition, July 18, 2007. Focusing on the family, parents are taught how to examine and understand their family's approach to food and body-image issues and its effect their child's behavior. Parents also learn how to identify an eating disorder in its early stages.

5. DYING TO BE THIN. By Ira Sacker and Marc Zimmer, Warner Books, Updated Edition June 2001. Understanding and defeating anorexia and bulimia.

6. WHEN YOUR CHILD HAS AN EATING DISORDER: A STEP BY STEP WORKBOOK FOR PARENTS AND OTHER CARE GIVERS. Abigail Natenshon, Jossey-Bass, 1999.

7. ANOREXIA NERVOSA: A GUIDE TO RECOVERY. Lindsey Hall and Monika Ostroff, Gurze Books, 1998

8. WASTED: A MEMOIR OF ANOREXIA AND BULIMIA. Marya Hornbacher, Harper Perennial, 1997

9. ANOREXIA NERVOSA: LET ME BE! A.H. Crisp, M.D., Routledge, April 19, 1995

10. THE BODY BETRAYED: A DEEPER UNDERSTANDING OF WOMEN, EATING DISORDERS, AND TREATMENT. Kathryn J. Zerbe, Gurze Books, 1995. Gives a deeper understanding of women, eating disorders and treatment. Delves into the full spectrum of factors contributing to eating disorders, such as family dynamics, cultural messages, nutrition, sexual abuse, and links with chemical dependency.

11. THE OBSESSION: RELFECTIONS ON THE TYRANNY OF SLENDERNESS: Kim Chernin, Harper & Collins, New York, Second Edition, 1994. Reflections on the tyranny of slenderness.

12. HUNGRY SELF: Women, Eating and Identity. Kim Chernin, Harper & Collins Inc., 1994. Deals with women, eating and identity.

13. FULL LIVES. Edited by Lindsey Hall, Gurze Books, 1993. Stories about women who have freed themselves from obsessions with food and weight.

14. TWELVE STEPS FOR OVEREATERS ANONYMOUS: AN INTERPRETATION OF THE TWELVE STEPS OF OVEREAYERS ANONYMOUS. Elisabeth L, Hazelden Publishing, 1993

15. BULIMAREXIA: The Binge Purge Cycle. Marlene Boskind-White, Ph.D., and William C. White, Jr., Ph.D., W.W. Norton and Company, Second Edition, 1991.

16. FASTING GIRLS: THE HISTORY OF ANOREXIA NERVOSA. Joan Jacobs Brumberg, Plume, Penguin Group, 1989. Explores historical roots from the fasting saints of the Middle Ages and the "fasting girls" of the Victorian Era to contemporary times.

17. MAKING PEACE WITH FOOD. Susan Kano, Harper Paperbacks, Revised edition, March 1, 1989. Step-by-step guide to overcoming repeated weight loss and gain, binge eating, guilt, and anxieties about food and body image.

18. TREATING AND OVERCOMING ANOREXIA NERVOSA. Steven Levenkron, M.D., Grand Central Publishing , April 5, 1988

19. TRANSFORMING BODY IMAGE: LOVE THE BODY YOU HAVE. Marcia Germaine Hutchinson, Ed.D., The Crossing Press, 1985. Talks about learning to love the body you have.

20. THE GOLDEN CAGE. By Hilde Bruch, M.D., Harvard University Press, 1978. Focuses on the enigma of anorexia nervosa.

21. EATING DISORDERS. Hilde Bruch, M.D., Basic Books, Inc., U.S., June 4, 1973. Talks about obesity, anorexia nervosa and the person within.

"FOOD" FOR THOUGHT RELATED TO EATING DISORDERS*

- One out of three women and one out of four men are on a diet at any given time.

- 35% of occasional dieters progress into pathological dieting.

- Two out of five women and one out of five men would trade three to five years of their life to achieve weight goals.

- Diet and diet-related products are a 33 billion dollar a year industry.

- One half of fourth grade girls are on a diet.

- 81% of ten year old girls are afraid of being fat.

- Frequent dieting is highly correlated with depression.

- Four out of Five U.S. women are dissatisfied with their appearance.

- When preschoolers were offered dolls identical in every respect except weight, they preferred the thin doll nine out of ten times.

- A study asked children to assign attractiveness values to pictures of children with various disabilities. Participants rated the obese child less attractive than a child in a wheelchair, a child with a facial deformity and a child with a missing limb.

- 50% of women wear size 14 or larger, but most standard clothing outlets cater to sizes 14 or smaller.

- The average U.S. woman is 5'4" and weighs 140 pounds. In contrast, the average U.S. model is 5'11" and weighs 117 pounds.

- Some of the pictures of the models in magazines do not really exist. The pictures are computer modified compilations of different body parts.

- Twenty years ago the average fashion model weighed 8% less than the average woman. Today she weighs 23% less.

- One out of every four TV commercials sends some sort of message about attractiveness.

- Marilyn Monroe set the beauty standard at 5'5" and 135 pounds. Today her agent would tell her she had to lose weight!

- In 1970 the average age a girl started dieting was 14; by 1990 the average age dropped to 8.

- A study fund that adolescent girls were more fearful of gaining weight than getting cancer, nuclear war, or losing their parents.

- In 1950 mannequins closely resembled the average measurements of women. The average hip measurement of mannequins and women were 34 inches. By 1990 the average woman's hip measurement was 37 inches, while the average mannequin's hip measured only 31 inches.

- Over the last three decades fashion models, Miss America contestants, and Playboy centerfolds have grown steadily thinner, while the average woman's weight has actually risen.

Information from Rader Treatment Programs specializing in Eating Disorders

Afterword

When I met Wendy in 1980, she was at the start of her journey to find health and recovery from anorexia nervosa. I was a pretty freshly-minted psychiatrist myself, and I was learning about anorexia as well. In 1977, the first eating disorders clinic in the country had just been opened at Massachusetts General Hospital where I had trained and where I was practicing. Over the next few years, Wendy and I learned a lot about the nightmare that anorexia can be, and how tenacious and seductive and irresistible the pull to starve can become.

I also learned that even when things were at their absolute worst for Wendy, she retained her unshakable integrity, her will to live, with an indomitable courage to carry on, to find a way. Her faith, her love of family and commitment to friends, and her openness to new experiences were crucial capabilities as she fought to establish a meaningful and satisfying life.

How anorexia happens was then and remains now something of a mystery. Why certain hurts cut into the heart, and awaken a terrible resolve to starve happens to some people and not to others—this was then and remains a mystery. Why some people become caught in the relentless cycle of starvation, trapped in the storm of fear and pride and desperate commitment that makes up this terrible disease— another mystery. But the paths to recovery are somewhat mysterious, too. People find recovery in all sorts of ways—some from treatment, some almost in spite of treatment. But one common element of recovery that has struck me is the sense of voice—recovery often involves the person's finding her own voice, and her right to a voice, and from that voice a right to a life.

As these pages so ably convey, Wendy indeed found her voice. Even as she wrestles again and again with the demons of anorexia, one senses the gathering force of her voice, maybe best exemplified when she left her unfulfilling marriage, and later when she left a relationship that was just not right for her. She spoke up for herself. She asserted her right to her own full life.

Reading this account of Wendy's struggle and her ultimate success in creating a life of dignity and meaning, with its share of romance, heartbreak, work, service, friends, and fulfillment humbles me and inspires me. That she has been willing to relive this struggle in these pages and use her writerly wisdom to capture the true experience of her journey is an act of profound generosity as well as creativity. May this book inspire others to carry on, find their own voice, and lay claim to a life of their own design.

Christopher Gordon, MD

Senior Vice President and Medical Director, Advocates

Associate Professor of Psychiatry, Part-time

Harvard Medical School

Acknowledgments

Revealing the "secrets" of my soul took a great deal of time, courage, and support. The process involved many starts and stops before I reached the finish line.

In addition to thanking Mya Kagan, my editor, I would also like to send a shout out to those who read my manuscript and provided feedback: Mari Broome, Chris Gordon, Howard Epstein, Marlene Epstein, Barry Levine, Anne Meyer, Mim Seidel, Ellen Seissian, Trisha Spina (of blessed memory), Kathleen Sullivan and Susan Wachter.

My heartfelt thanks to Mari Broome and Chris Gordon, for not only writing the foreword and afterword, but also for helping me carve out and live a life despite the encumbrance of anorexia nervosa. Thanks to Fairwinds Treatment Center as well as other therapists including Alan Feldman, M.D., who helped me along the way. Also, thanks to NEDA for allowing me to use information from their website.

Special thanks to Ellen Seissian, Kathleen Sullivan, and Susan Wachter for their candid comments which appear on the back cover.

Last but not least, thanks to my dear friend and superb graphic artist, Anne Meyer, whose talent made my book's cover come to life!

Made in the USA
Monee, IL
01 April 2025

15013706R00094